I JUST WANT IT TO WORK!

A Guide to Understanding Digital
Marketing and Social Media for Frustrated
Business Owners, Managers and Marketers

KEVIN SPITERI

As someone who works with thousands upon thousands of business owners every year, I think it's fair to say we are all frustrated. The transition into a digital world has not been smooth sailing for all, especially when it comes to digital marketing and social media. I think that Kevin Spiteri gets this better than most – and his wonderful new book *I Just Want It To Work!* provides the hope of sanity for all of us. A great read, smart, well thought out, and I now feel far more hopeful about surviving in a digital world.

Andrew Griffiths, Australia's #1 Small Business and
Entrepreneurial Author

In the complicated world of modern marketing, underpinned by digital and social media, Kevin takes tech and helps break it down in layman's terms. We had the pleasure of engaging Kevin and his tech company to develop an industry-leading website platform, which allows us to provide our customers around Australia with a clean, professional, and modern website that takes no more than five minutes to update. Our dealings with Kevin have been enlightening and helpful, to say the least, in deciding on the best and most appropriate strategy to explore at any given time.

Damien Hill, General Manager Sales & Marketing,
Burson Automotive, www.burson.com.au

I take great satisfaction in writing this testimony for Kevin Spiteri. We were introduced to Kevin through my accountant, whilst in the process of setting up a merchandise brand and all-purpose training and fitness website.

Not only did Kevin help set the strategic and creative direction for our brand, our online presence and digital marketing, he helped ensure our website was first-class, and was extremely hands on in maintaining the end result once completed.

His easy, non-flustered and strategic approach was exactly what my business partner and I were looking for and it paid dividends.

I wouldn't hesitate in recommending Kevin for any venture you would choose to engage him on.

Mark Geyer, OAM, Director, Wild Panther Fitness, Triple M Grill Team host and ex–Penrith Panthers Rugby League player

Kevin has been at the forefront of DBC2's digital marketing offer for the past four years, and has been the linchpin to it becoming the most important division in our agency. It was Kevin's commitment to developing a sound structure that delivered real results to our clients and took DBC2 from being just a player to becoming an industry leader.

What sets Kevin apart from the rest is his insatiable appetite for improvement. There is never a day that he sits still reflecting on how good things are – he is always looking for the next best way. This has always given me the confidence that we are delivering the best for our clients.

In our industry, it's vital to put complex marketing into layman's terms and map out clear and easy-to-understand strategy. Kevin has mastered this. He understands the need for clients to feel there is going to be ROI on their digital investment, and right from the start he develops a sense of trust by talking in their language.

Dale Brittain, Managing Director, DBC2, Australia's Automotive Marketing Specialists, www.dbc2.com.au

We are in the early stages of our relationship with Kevin and his team, but so far we are very impressed with his methodical approach to strategy and the depth and breadth of his knowledge. Kevin has a fantastic ability to take complex concepts relating to digital marketing and social media and break them down and explain them in layman's terms. We are excited about implementing the digital marketing strategy that he has recommended for our business.

Damien Wilde, Director, Henry Kendall Group,
www.henrykendall.com.au

Kevin takes strategic thinking to a new level. We often bring Kevin a series of marketing problems, ideas and questions, and within a single meeting he is able to distil and understand all of them. With his vast and diverse experience, he ties together a mishmash of inputs in a unified strategy. His feedback often dramatically improves initial ideas and is regularly supplemented with detailed implementation methods. His passion and enthusiasm is contagious, which keeps us coming back for more.

Stephen Bartlett, CEO, The Audio Hunt, www.theaudiohunt.com

Having engaged Kevin and his team for almost three years now, we have had the pleasure of growing our business as Kevin has grown his. Kevin has been fundamental in the growth and development of our digital and social presence. Online and digital now accounts for 50% of our business, and we value Kevin's insight, education and genuine interest in helping ensure our go-to-market strategy is sound.

Dallas Simmonds, General Manager, Titan Enterprises (Incorporating Titan Garages and Sheds, Titan Lite and ARD Garage Doors),
www.titangarages.com.au

First published in 2017 by Kevin Spiteri
www.kevinaspiteri.com.au

National Library of Australia Cataloguing-in-Publication entry:

Creator: Spiteri, Kevin, author.

Title: I just want it to work!: A guide to understanding digital marketing and social media for frustrated business owners, managers and marketers / Kevin Spiteri.

ISBN: 9780648018049 (paperback)

Subjects: Internet marketing – Australia – Handbooks, manuals, etc.
Social media – Marketing – Handbooks, manuals, etc.
Online social networks in business – Handbooks, manuals, etc.
Electronic commerce – Handbooks, manuals, etc.

Project management and text design by Michael Hanrahan Publishing
Cover design by Peter Reardon
Cover icons designed by Freepik

The paper this book is printed on is certified as environmentally friendly.

Disclaimer

CONTENTS

Foreword *by Jordan Grives* *xiii*

Introduction: So, you're a little bit frustrated ... **1**
Good thing you found this book ... 2
So, who am I? 3
Watching businesses grow 7

PART I: LET'S HAVE A CUPPA

1. **Problems, problems, problems** **11**
You are not alone 12
The three dominant problems 14
Why are you doing this? 16

2. **The importance of clear objectives** **19**
Drilling down 19
Time to get SMART 20

3. **Myriad mistakes: want a cuddle?** **29**
The most common digital marketing and social mistakes 31
A checkpoint 40

4.   The truth? You can't handle the truth! (Or can you?)   43
Choosing the right agency for your business   44
The truth about the agency   45
The truth about your business   46
A checkpoint   46

5.   Understanding the universal language of marketing   49
What *is* marketing?   49
Who are you selling to?   49
Marketing transcends industries   51
Profiling methodology   52
A checkpoint   53

PART II: UNDERSTANDING DIGITAL MARKETING AND SOCIAL MEDIA OBJECTIVES FOR YOUR BUSINESS

6.   It's more than just sales   57
That was then   57
This is now   58
Is marketing responsible for sales?   58
The key objectives   58
Paid, owned, earned   59
A checkpoint   61

7.   Understanding brand awareness   63
The difficulties of measuring brand awareness   63
Today, content is king   65
Content clarified   68
A checkpoint   72

8.   Understanding lead generation   75
Sowing the right seeds   76
Highly qualified and targeted leads   77
Handy things to know   79
A checkpoint   81

9.   Understanding engagement and community   83
Communication is no longer one way   83
Free market research   84
Your customers now have more power   85
Just about *everybody* is on social media   88
More than just a two-way dialogue   90
Real-world communities still matter   93
A checkpoint   93

10. Understanding traffic   95
Monitoring and understanding your traffic   96
A checkpoint   100

PART III: BUDGETING (SHOW ME THE MONEY!)

11. Talking about money   105
Investing in your business   105
Establishing certainty, accountability and value   106
Handy things to know   109
A checkpoint   109

12. How much should I invest?   111
Where should I invest my money?   112
Finding the best strategy for you   112
A checkpoint   114

13. Calculating return on investment 117
Objectives and ROI   117
Crunching the numbers   121
Getting the whole picture   124
A checkpoint   125

PART IV: THE SIX STEPS FOR SUCCESS (HERD SHEEP NOT CATS)

14. Step 1: Analyse 129
Gathering the data   130
Diving into the data   133
A checkpoint   133

15. Step 2: Strategise 135
Getting down to business   136
Sticking to your guns   139
A checkpoint   140

16. Step 3: Create 143
Your website   144
Facebook   145
LinkedIn   147
Instagram   148
Google   148
Electronic direct mail   155
Summary of the purpose of each platform   156
A checkpoint   158

17. Step 4: Implement 161
Handy things to know   162
A checkpoint   163

18. Step 5: Measure 165
Tools for measuring online activity 166
Understanding the results 167
The bigger picture 168
A checkpoint 169

19. Step 6: Refine 171
The back-end work 172
Keeping it simple 177
A checkpoint 177

PART V: EXECUTION (READY, AIM, FIRE)

20. The follow through 181
Where to now? 182
A checkpoint 184

Acknowledgements 193
Index 197

FOREWORD

Kevin Spiteri and I met back in 2010: Kevin happened to be head of marketing for one of the large Fortune 500 companies I was trying to procure services from. We spoke on and off for about 18 months, and throughout these dealings he was always courteous, understanding and genuine, which made me think that I might have better success with my businesses if I could get a face-to-face with him.

From the time I first met Kevin, I was astounded by the way he conducted himself. His business acumen was both polished and invigorating; I immediately knew that he not only had a solid insight into the industries in which he worked, but he also had a keen interest in and understanding of a wide range of commerce. Even though Kevin was responsible for the marketing of a company with $180 million revenue and 75 franchisees, our first short, half-hour meeting stretched out for over two hours.

The genuine and honest nature in which Kevin presented was nothing less than refreshing. Watching him allow his team to feel part of the decision-making process was also admirable, and not something that I had come across often within my own industry. He focused on the overall strategy and was open to listening to alternatives to his preferred approach for the product I was selling.

Fast-forward a few months, and after some intense negotiations and extreme attention to detail, we had managed to get a deal completed and we were in business. During this time my business was on a very quick growth trajectory, which was adding internal pressures. It can be difficult to trust people to share your pains with and seek advice professionally. Kevin, however, was someone I immediately felt at ease with, and over time he became a friend and confidant.

From that period on, we've shared many lunches and dinners where we can both openly discuss our ideas or issues that are going on within our professional or personal lives. We particularly enjoy opening a bottle or two of Kevin's carefully selected wines and discussing how we will solve all our problems.

It's very hard to describe a relationship with someone accurately in writing, but to this day, Kevin is the type of person who will always be engaged and invested in what you're saying and always offers an unbiased view.

When it comes to marketing, particularly in digital and social media, it's a complicated world – sometimes a little too complicated. My experience with most marketers is that they tend to focus on their interests and strengths, as opposed to broadening their horizons and looking at the next wave of technology. Kevin is the authority in this space. His education and experience, combined with his sound business acumen and an intimate knowledge of modern marketing, position him perfectly to author this book.

With his extreme attention to detail, Kevin thinks about every angle and always has return on investment at the top of his mind (which for me is one of the most important attributes). Whenever it comes to strategy, in my professional and personal opinion Kevin is the man to speak to.

Jordan Grives
CEO/Founder

Jordan Grives is one of Australia's youngest and most talented entrepreneurs. Having founded telco start-up Fonebox and built it into a $10 million-plus company, he successfully sold it to Nasdaq-listed j2 Global in late 2016.

Jordan is an esteemed professional in the space, having been the recipient of awards including Young Entrepreneur of the Year (2015 Brisbane), EY Entrepreneur of the Year (national finalist), the Deloitte Technology Fast 50, BRW Fast Starters and Smart50. He has been featured in *Smart Company*, *BRW*, *Anthill* and more.

Jordan now is the founder of Capital J Investments, a private fund designed to invest in an array of companies. He is also Executive Chairman of Fone Dynamics, and co-founder of Alicorn Ventures, a newly established Brisbane-based incubator designed to fuel high-growth tech companies, open to a wide array of industry verticals.

www.capitaljinvestments.com

SO, YOU'RE A LITTLE BIT FRUSTRATED ...

Do your eyes glaze over when somebody mentions "marketing" or "social media"? Do you know it's important for the success of your business, but you'd rather poke yourself in the eye with a stick than spend time and money "messing around with that stuff"? Are you a frustrated business owner, manager or marketer who's a little lost in the digital web?

Perhaps you have dabbled in it a little, or at least made an attempt to get involved, but feel frustrated as your time, energy and money invested haven't produced the results you've expected? Or perhaps you may be a little further ahead and have gone down the path of engaging a third party or employing an internal resource, and you feel self-conscious that you don't know the right questions to ask, or how to hold them accountable for their actions?

Alternatively, you may be frustrated because you feel you've had a piecemeal approach to marketing, things seem somewhat disjointed, and you look to other brands, businesses and even your competitors with envy because they seem to have it together.

You may be confused by the myriad resources out there on the topic, or about where to start or knowing what may be best for you and your business. You may be overwhelmed with advice from friends, family, colleagues, the next-door neighbour or other business owners who each have particular ideas about how you should be marketing your business in the digital and social space.

GOOD THING YOU FOUND THIS BOOK ...

If that sounds like you, congratulations – you're in the right place! Solving these problems is what I live for.

In this book we're going to look at the major facets of all things digital and social media, using a strategic marketing approach to understand the best way to attack this part of your business. The *strategic marketing approach* is what is key here. All too often I see businesses that jump straight to the tactics (we cover why this is dangerous) and they attempt to go direct to specialist or individual providers for the various components of their digital and social marketing, only to realise how unmanageable this approach is due to the difficulty of someone in the business trying to pull it all together and manage multiple vendors.

I am going to help you make sense of the different aspects, explain how they all relate, and pull those pieces of the digital and social puzzle together for you, while showing you how to ensure you not only set the right objectives but ensure they just *work* for you and your business.

I aim to cut out the bull. I want you to feel that you are sitting down with me, having a coffee (or a glass of wine) and I'm talking you through each component in a really simple, easy-to-understand and jargon-free way. I intend to ensure that you can avoid the many pieces of advice from well-meaning people who tell you that "you need to implement [insert almost any tactic] in your business", and enable you to make your own choices for you and your unique business.

You will walk away from this book with absolute confidence and with enough knowledge to become dangerous, to ask the right questions, and hold either your internal team or a third-party agency accountable for their strategies and tactics.

I believe it's your obligation as a business owner to understand all things marketing, digital and social. That doesn't mean that you need to know the intricacies or even how to do it yourself, but you have an obligation to know enough to ensure you're making the best decisions for your business. Just like finance, business owners and directors are responsible for the numbers and are liable for business performance – marketing, digital and social are no different.

I am genuinely excited by what I hope you are going to take from this book, even if it's only a few key learnings that help govern your strategy moving forward, or perhaps a more holistic approach where you ensure whomever is responsible for this function within your business is accountable for what they are tasked with executing.

How to get the most out of this book

To get the most out of this book, read and re-read chapters. Skip ahead to the topics that interest you if you are trying to make some decisions, and use the notes pages in each chapter to write a few key points that are relevant to your business and how the chapter could help you.

SO, WHO AM I?

You're reading my book, so it's only fair I tell you a little bit about who I am and how I came to write *I Just Want It To Work!* Born in 1982, and growing up in a blue-collar family in various suburbs of Campbelltown, in Western Sydney, I never imagined I would become an entrepreneur or successful business owner. Heck, I didn't even really know what an "entrepreneur" was, let alone dared to call myself one.

So how then did I become an experienced marketer? A successful business owner? An entrepreneur? An investor and owner of a number of start-ups? A mentor? An author?

Hard work

Well, I started young. I witnessed my father working incredibly hard every single day, six (and at times, seven) days a week (overtime was the "holy grail"). He was a craftsman. A shopfitter and joiner by trade, his skills were impeccable; what I saw him build, create, conceptualise and deliver taught me more than I realised at the time. Work ethic, creativity, taking pride in your work, problem solving and resilience were all valuable lessons that contributed to my journey.

My mother on the other hand was an academic, who valued education, yet chose to be a wonderful stay at home mother who would ensure she was there for us every single day, yet this made for a very modest upbringing.

We didn't really know what this meant until we were older. When I was around eight years old it started to become evident. We didn't have the latest toys or brand-name clothes, we didn't go on holidays, nor did we go to the Sydney Royal Easter Show. I recall watching my mother on Friday nights, taking my dad's small yellow envelope which had his pay in it, and dividing it up into the usual groups: food, utilities, school, clothes, and so on. Needless to say there wasn't much left at the end of each week. Don't get me wrong; we always had a roof over our head, food on the table, clothes on our back and an education, but we didn't have much more than the necessities of life.

I quickly realised two things. The first was that if I wanted holidays, brand-name clothes and the latest gadgets I was going to have to work for them; and secondly, I realised that I *did* want to have nice things, because to me they were representative of hard work.

I was hungry for success.

My first job and my first business

Just shy of 14 years old, I got my first job working at a supermarket – from the cash register to trolley boy, I did it all. I learned valuable lessons about customer service, how to relate to people and help people, working in teams, and the value of working for my money, so much so that I went out and got a second job.

While earning $5 an hour seemed okay, I wanted more. This is when I started my first business: car stereo installations.

I had a thing for electronics, having played with electronic kits that were purchased secondhand from the markets. I figured out circuitry and had a fair idea how it all worked. Using my older sister's car as a guinea pig, I managed to figure out how to install a head-unit and a set of speakers. Thankfully it worked just fine, so I started telling people I knew that I could install car stereos. Word got around, and from my parents' garage and front driveway my first "business" began (much to the annoyance of my neighbours when the "doof, doof" started – sorry Mr Wilson).

It quickly reached the point where people started asking for quotes. I told them to get a quote from a well-known professional car stereo retail chain (which is no longer around), and promised them that I would beat the installation quote by 50%! (The joy of no overheads.) Soon I was being asked if I could select and purchase the gear on behalf of my customers, and after developing a relationship with another car stereo retail chain, I was able to buy the equipment for them at a discounted rate. Before long, the installations became more complex, and people started asking for customised work, so I then started "sub-contracting" my dad to make the sub-woofer boxes for my customers.

I didn't know it at the time but I was learning valuable marketing lessons: the power of word of mouth, the importance of being competitive, the importance of partnerships and collaboration, the importance of engaging the appropriate skills, and finding people with complementary products, skills or services.

By the age of 20 I stopped installing car stereos. I had successfully funded everything in my life from the age of 14: my car, my toys, a dirt bike, brand-name clothes, going out money, awesome

Christmas presents for my siblings (you're welcome) … well, you get the picture.

What's a Toolmaker?

But, this is not even where my career began. In fact, I'm a Toolmaker by trade. A Toolmaker you ask!? Many of you reading this book may not even know what one is.

When I used to tell people I was a Toolmaker, they thought I made hammers and screwdrivers. I won't go into too much detail, suffice to say it's effectively a mechanical engineering trade, where you manufacture "tools" that create things; for example, moulds that manufacture plastic components, or press tools that "stamp" metal to form it into shapes. It is a trade of perfection, working to the finest of tolerances, the ultimate in precision.

This is where my marketing career actually began.

Having barely worked for long on the factory floor, the Director of the company I worked for at the time must have seen something in me (or perhaps he just thought I was a terrible Toolmaker!), and he asked if I would be interested in encouraging other young people who were at school to become a Toolmaker/Engineer too by exhibiting at a career expo. Sure enough, I put together a display, gathered some brochures and some cool samples of things we made, and off I went to the exhibit.

There my love of marketing began, as did my career shift, and my education. And for the next 14 years I went on to study and receive a multitude of undergrad and post grad qualifications in business, marketing and finally an MBA (Master of Business Administration). When I reflect on why this led to a career change, I think it became evident to me really early on that my mind, my personality, and my interests resonated with the marketing field. I have always been a mix of creative and strategic, with an artistic flair, but with an analytical mind (over-analytical at times). What's more, I loved every minute of it. The challenges, the strategies, the diversity in day-to-day operations all appealed to me. I loved knowing that I was at the forefront of things, usually before anyone else even knew about something.

WATCHING BUSINESSES GROW

Ultimately my career has enabled me to watch businesses grow. I have had the opportunity to work both client side and agency side. I have been responsible for the tiniest of budgets within start-ups and the most lucrative of budgets in the corporate world.

What I genuinely hope is, regardless of where you are in the business spectrum, you take something useful away from this book. Whether you are a start-up investing personal funds into your business while you bootstrap a minimum viable product (MVP) through to a marketing manager, senior manager or owner, founder, or director of a much larger, more established organisation with a healthy budget to allocate towards your activities, this book will give you insight to help either direct your marketing strategies or to be armed with the knowledge required to engage professionals to support you with your digital marketing and social media activities.

My objective is to help you overcome a lack of knowledge and common misunderstandings the world of digital marketing tends to bring with it these days. My objective is to make you feel confident and comfortable with your decisions moving forward, and most importantly, to know that you are making the soundest of investments with your eyes wide open.

I wish you all the best with your digital marketing and social media activities.

Kevin Spiteri, 2017
www.kevinaspiteri.com.au

NOTES:

PART I

LET'S HAVE
A CUPPA

1

PROBLEMS, PROBLEMS, PROBLEMS

Every single day I am contacted by existing or potential clients who are seeking answers to the problems, challenges and difficulties they face on a day-to-day basis when it comes to their marketing, digital or social media.

As someone who is responsible for overseeing these functions for many businesses, I've heard all the concerns you most likely have, all the problems and all the challenges you face. There are very few times when I sit in front of a client and their marketing challenge knocks me for six. Don't get me wrong; I am certainly not saying I know it all, nor do I profess to have all the answers, but what I do understand is that many of the challenges posed to me typically relate to a few common areas.

Often a client will call and be near frantic about an issue such as:

- a competitor is launching an aggressive campaign against them online

- a new entrant to the market has taken them by surprise and they don't know what to do

- their budget is under scrutiny and they are concerned about where to invest money to yield the best returns

- they feel they don't have adequate resources to address a core marketing function within the organisation and need scalable support to do so.

There are many other issues I could add to this list, and I've seen them all before.

YOU ARE NOT ALONE

Sometimes it's easy to feel like you are alone. It's easy to feel that you are the only person or the only business that faces the kinds of problems you're having.

Do you sometimes stop and ask why you don't know more about things like digital marketing or social media? Perhaps you've felt a sense of guilt that, as things change, your focus on your business or career has meant that you have struggled to keep up to date with the latest technology, trends, techniques, methodologies and strategies? Perhaps it interests you so little that you've felt your current efforts in business were sustainable, and that having to do anything different was somewhat unnecessary?

I take it for granted that you are already excellent at what you do in the business you own or are responsible for. You know your clients, you understand what's important to them; perhaps you've built your entire reputation on word of mouth? Perhaps you've always managed to service a small, local market, and that has always worked well. Maybe you've found that going to networking events, joining industry associations or simply handing out some fliers has sufficed in generating enough business. Or perhaps you have worked in a "traditional" industry which has yielded great returns.

But perhaps now things have changed. New competitors have entered the market. Your market or industry is now being disrupted through new technologies, new behaviours and changes in the way your audience interacts with your business and your competition.

Seemingly overnight, you're competing against not only national businesses but international ones as well. These new competitors are using myriad platforms to market themselves, they have a killer website, they are on Facebook, Instagram and YouTube (or any of the plethora of other digital and social media channels), and wherever you seem to go on the internet they seem to follow you around with their ads. Or you might even have signed up (with your fake name and pseudo email account) to find out what kind of information you will receive from them through the website, and now you are getting weekly offers, news and events?

Alternatively, you may well even be across some of these things. You've forked out some money for a website, you've dabbled with a bit of Facebook, perhaps even chucked an ad up on Google to "see what happens"? It seems no matter what you do though, there is still an element of frustration, derived from the outcome being unsatisfactory, or from not knowing what is the most ideal or most effective strategy for your business, or from not knowing who you can trust and who can genuinely help your business.

I want you to know that you are not alone. In fact, having worked with hundreds of businesses, and having interviewed many of them, I know that their problems, while often articulated in slightly different ways, all carried very similar themes.

THE THREE DOMINANT PROBLEMS

The businesses I've worked with over the years have three dominant problems when it comes to their digital marketing and social media:

- money

- uncertainty

- resources.

Let's have a look at each of these.

Problem #1: Money

In my experience, money tends to become a "chicken or the egg" discussion with businesses. In other words, most of the businesses we work with are already making money doing what they do, they are successful in their own right, however they are aware they need to invest money in marketing in order to make more money or to deliver a number of other objectives (see chapter 2).

The question though is not only *where* to invest that money, but *how* to best invest the money. No doubt you can already relate to many other business owners out there who are simply concerned about the value for money they will get when they invest into digital marketing and social media. You may also be uncertain as to how much you should invest: how much is too much, or how little is too little? (We'll consider that later in the book.)

Ultimately I've learnt businesses want one thing when it comes to their investment: *results*. You want your investment to be focused and accountable. You want to know your investment is being allocated in the most strategic of ways, giving it the ultimate opportunity for success. You want to know exactly where your money is being allocated and why it's being allocated in that manner.

Problem #2: Uncertainty

In speaking to so many business owners over the years, I know that the one thing they yearn for when it comes to their digital marketing and social media is certainty. Undoubtedly that's what you are looking for as well. Certainty you are making the most strategic decisions, certainty your money is being invested into the appropriate platforms, certainty you will derive positive results from your efforts, and certainty that all of the deliverables will be … delivered!

Uncertainty can be derived from a number of areas: it could be a lack of knowledge or education about the most up-to-date digital marketing and social media tools, techniques, methods and technologies. It could be that you have tried a particular path before that was unsuccessful for you. It could be financial – you may be uncertain about whether your investment is going to be enough to make things work, or uncertain about how long it will take, or uncertain about the results you will yield. The list is long.

My aim is to help you overcome this uncertainty when it comes to digital marketing and social media.

Problem #3: Resources

It doesn't matter what size business you are, resources are always going to seem scarce. And the resources you allocate and invest in are typically going to be linked to the core functions relating to the delivery of your business's core product or service.

For those who have been in business for many years, you would recall that for the majority of SMEs (small to medium enterprises), placing an ad in the *Yellow Pages* with the help of their in-house graphic design team, or going to your local printer to have some business cards or flyers made up, and perhaps – for some – heading to your local radio station to have them record and place advertisements for you was enough; in fact, it was more than enough to grow a business.

Many of the "mainstream" media advertising methods (or as marketers call them, "above the line": television, print and radio) are or were quite cost prohibitive for SMEs. What's more, because these approaches reach mass audiences you would be exposed to waste, and so it was traditionally difficult to truly gauge the success of your efforts.

This problem of resources tends to compound when it comes to digital marketing and social media in business today. Nowadays there are a number of ways in which you can relate to and engage with your target customer. With so many "free" online platforms out there, the barriers to entry for developing a website, getting a logo designed, starting a social media page and sending out email marketing are now extremely low. In fact, you could do almost everything required to get the basics right yourself for free or with very little cost.

Enter the problem of resources. Business owners are now torn about how much they should do themselves, or question if any of it should be outsourced. The value equation then comes into play, and because many of the methods are low cost or free, business owners tend to grapple with the cost versus the return, and often are willing to spend more of their most precious resource (time) on doing it themselves. Most quickly realise this is unsustainable.

WHY ARE YOU DOING THIS?

Ultimately, all of these issues come back to one simple thing: objectives. Once you know what your objectives are for your online marketing, you will be able to make educated, informed and calculated decisions for your business and its digital and social media efforts. Use the notes section to identify how you can relate to the three dominant problems and identify your concerns.

NOTES:

NOTES:

2

THE IMPORTANCE OF CLEAR OBJECTIVES

When first exploring digital marketing and social media, it's okay to not necessarily know exactly what you want to achieve. Many business owners simply start out with ideas such as "I want more sales", or "I just want the phone to ring", or "I want people to talk about my company". This is fine to get you started, but if you want to achieve remarkable results and ongoing success with your digital marketing and social media strategy, you'll have to move beyond these generic goals to create meaningful objectives for your business.

So, let's see how you can do that!

DRILLING DOWN

Let's assume that by this point in the book you have already acknowledged that trying to do it yourself is not quite going to work. Now, whether you choose to employ an internal marketing resource or engage a third party doesn't really matter. What matters is that it's a marketer's role – internal or external – to help get really clear and drill down on *exactly* what you as the business owner or manager are looking for. They should know the right questions to ask to unpack and extract exactly what your business needs at that point in time.

It's easy to "want it all", to feel that your product or your service caters to or can serve everyone. That may well be true, but that's not going to give you a good starting point for a campaign. If you had to rein it in a little, what would your ideal target market be? Who do you feel you can serve the best or who is your product or service best suited to?

This is the starting point of a successful marketing campaign. Getting really clear on your specific audience – and not only what you want to get out of them, but more importantly knowing where you can add the most value to them – is critical to ensuring three things:

- your budget goes further
- your message is relevant to your specific audience
- your efforts are rewarded in the results you obtain.

TIME TO GET SMART

One thing I often find that helps to clarify these issues and set the foundations for objective setting is to use the old SMART principle: Specific, Measurable, Attainable, Relevant and Realistic, Timely. (We cover specific objectives related to digital marketing and social media in part II.)

Specific

I've seen and worked with many businesses that find being specific really difficult. Honestly, I don't blame them most of the time. After all, many of them have products and services that could be used by or appeal to just about anybody.

I recall meeting with a client once who had an e-tail business (online shop) selling car parts. Our first conversation revolved around trying to understand exactly who their website was best suited for. In other words, where they could focus to yield the best immediate results to drive sustainable revenue with medium to high profit transactions while building their database (there's a big hint there about how to help focus and become really specific).

So I asked these questions:

- "Was their offering for someone who was a car enthusiast, who knew their stuff, knew what they were looking for and wanted the best service, convenient purchasing and rapid delivery?"

- "Was their offering for the new car owner who was looking for some accessories such as car seat covers?"

- "Was their offering for an aware buyer who was simply doing research trying to find the best price for the product they were after?"

When we drilled down into it, the key products and target audience were identified as "car accessories", primarily for young women (18 to 25) who had specific types of cars (such as hatchbacks and small sedans), who lived on the outskirts of CBDs. The site made the selection of accessories for a vehicle super simple with a really powerful vehicle search tool. Women within that category are among the most prolific users and consumers of online purchasing. Experience also showed they had a tendency to become intimidated when walking into retailers and asking for advice on the accessories they were after.

This is the key to being specific: you must *drill down* into who the key target market is. "Car owners", "home owners" or "people who like sport" are simply not specific enough.

What types of cars? How much do they spend on them? How old are the cars? What makes? Where do these people live?

What types of homes? What locations? How many people live in them? How big are the homes?

What sports? Are you after participants or spectators? What age groups? What skill level: beginners or experts?

These types of questions are just the beginning, and you should be updating your questions and data on your target market regularly. Focus is the key to success when it comes to your digital marketing and social media efforts.

Measurable

If you can't measure the effectiveness of your set objective, and more so the outcome of your activity that is focused on that objective, how will you know if it's succeeded? The beauty about working the digital and social space now is our ability to measure everything. Even in its simplest form, without getting too technical or over-complicating things, you can reliably measure the effectiveness of your efforts and assess them against the objectives you have set.

In the instance of the online car parts business, while sales of course were valuable rewards for their efforts, what was more valuable was being able to segment a very specific target audience (women, with small cars, aged 18 to 25, who lived on the outskirts of CBDs). Through digital campaigns, this very specific audience was able to be targeted, and once the data was collected and the database was generated, it soon became evident that they were in fact reaching the right people. Gathering their data either during the interest phase or the purchase phase meant the business could confirm that they were targeting the correct audience. The databases of these key markets become an asset for the business.

(In part IV we examine how to track a campaign; at this stage it's just important for you to know that you must establish some goals that can be tracked.)

Attainable

Setting an objective becomes the foundation of your marketing strategy, which results in the determination of your digital marketing and social media tactics. It also determines the best channels, methods and processes required to achieve it. However, if the objective is "unattainable" then no matter what you do you will ultimately be disappointed with the outcome.

It's important that you ensure your objective is attainable. As a business owner you will weigh up the risks involved, and determine if what you are looking to achieve is going to be possible given the timeframe, budget and resources at hand. Even in its simplest form, for example, you may have an objective to build a database of 10,000 people. But you may only have a budget of $500. Basic mathematics in this instance demonstrates that each person in the database would need to come at a cost of $0.05 (five cents each), and most of you would understand that the chances of building a qualified database with your target audience at five cents a lead would be remote. Of course, this is a bit of an exaggeration, but it helps to illustrate the point so that you can manage your expectations.

An unattainable objective might be to get one million hits on your website next month; an attainable objective might be to get 20,000 hits. An unattainable objective might be to triple your revenue in three months. An attainable objective might be to increase your revenue by 40% in that time.

Don't by any means let this discourage you from having big goals and setting ambitious objectives, just be mindful and put a little bit of thought into what it might mean when it's time to execute.

An unattainable objective can actually thwart your efforts as you'll become discouraged when you realise it won't be achieved.

Realistic and relevant

This might sound like an obvious one, but it's amazing how many businesses I have spoken to who consider setting objectives that are unrealistic and irrelevant to their core business or their core market. It seems many businesses tend to be great and do a particular thing really well, yet when it comes to wanting to embark on digital marketing or social media strategies, the focus tends to be on something pretty left of centre or out of the usual realm of their business.

A desire to do more as a business, or to branch out, is healthy, yet often we see that when a business simply focuses on being excellent at just one main thing, in one primary market, and being the best they can be in their space, it becomes more stable. Amplifying this stability through their marketing and digital efforts ultimately results in more profit and greater demand. The best bit about achieving this *first* is that it then opens up the revenue stream to allow for branching out, making that transition into new or untapped markets, and entering a space that is less relevant to the business at its current point.

As such, being realistic in the goal setting ensures you aren't setting yourself up for failure. As mentioned under the "attainable" section, setting expectations that are misaligned with your budget, or worse, setting growth expectations that are beyond either your ability to scale or service, is a recipe for disaster. Sounds like common sense but it is often overlooked. There is immense value in the long game here: conservative, considered and consistent growth over a sustained period. So make your objectives realistic and relevant to what you are doing.

Timely

Deadlines mean things get done.

Without a timeline to execute and achieve your objective, it will become easy to digress, or worse, cut things short or go for too long.

Similar to being attainable, the timeframe in which you set your objective will be determined by the channels, methods and processes. For example, if you decided a direct marketing strategy was required to achieve your objective and you gave the campaign one week, it is unlikely that you will meet your objective or give it the appropriate time to generate results. It may even be physically impossible to do everything that is required to build and execute the strategy within that timeframe.

To help you establish timeframes (keeping in mind these are general guidelines based on my experience working with clients across multiple industries), consider the following:

- **Marketing strategies:** these should be set on average six months to a year in advance.

- **Digital strategies/campaigns:** most of these tend to yield the best results when executed for at least a three-month period. Often what is overlooked here is the need for ongoing refinement and tweaking in order to optimise the campaigns to be most effective. Many of the digital platforms require that data be accumulated in order to improve and optimise; this data is only acquired over time and is based on people's online behaviour.

- **Social strategies:** if the decision is made as an organisation to engage in a considered social media strategy then you need to be willing to commit for the long term (12 to 24 months minimum). While this is covered in more detail in chapter 6, social media should be seen as a marketing channel for your business, and a way of creating interesting, engaging and meaningful relationships with your target audience. Like any relationship, this takes time.

Hopefully you are beginning to feel a little more comfortable about what you have done or are planning to do moving forward when it comes to objective setting. As you can see there is no need to over-complicate things. The simpler the better.

The objective for this chapter is to give yourself the time to think through 'how' you're setting your SMART objectives to be of value to the organisation. Use the notes section at the end of this chapter to start developing some SMART objectives for your marketing, digital campaigns or social media strategies.

NOTES:

NOTES:

3

MYRIAD MISTAKES: WANT A CUDDLE?

We all make mistakes. Heck, most of what I've achieved as a marketer may not have been possible without making some mistakes along the way. I've been responsible for "not getting it", I've been guilty of trying "the cheapest", conversely I've even wasted money on the wrong marketing strategies, I've made decisions without the appropriate research, and I've made poor decisions because I've rushed into things.

But mistakes are okay – if you learn from them.

My team members and past employees will attest to a philosophy I've always had: regardless of the "cost" of the mistake (as it's usually reflective of the size and type of business), making the mistake is actually an investment in your education. I'm sure some might disagree, and many businesses would argue that making mistakes can be very problematic and cause a business to go under. Well I am here to argue that if you have put all your eggs into one basket, and that basket turns out to be a mistake, then you need to own the decision of putting all your eggs in the one basket in the first place. That's the mistake – not what went wrong later.

If this were a workshop or a conference where I was speaking to established business owners and managers, I would ask the following questions:

Consider these questions …

- Have you spent money on marketing activities that haven't worked?

For those who have answered that question in their head with "YES", then ask yourself if …

- you tried a single strategy that was "guaranteed" to solve all of your problems

- you took the advice of a friend or family member on what they thought would be the best marketing strategy for your business

- you believed what you were looking for could easily be compared in terms of price (for example, you obtained three quotes and you would try to compare apples with apples)

- you were presented with a series of options and you went with the cheapest one based solely on price

- you were persuaded by a sales call to make the decision.

Lastly, ask yourself if you did or didn't understand where or why you went wrong with these marketing strategies.

The point of this exercise is to not only reflect and learn about what you have or haven't done, but also to ascertain the reasons behind why things may not have worked to your expectations. Often in the industry someone will attempt a marketing, digital or social strategy, give it one month, and then say, "Well, it didn't work so I'm never going to do that again." You must take ownership of a failed campaign and make a point of understanding why it didn't work.

Again, you're not alone. I interviewed over 40 established businesses across multiple industries before writing this book to establish the mistakes they have made when it came to their digital marketing and social media activity. What I found was quite interesting: that many of these businesses, regardless of industry, had a tendency to make very similar, if not the same, mistakes.

These mistakes can be broken down into two areas: thinking mistakes (the things in business the owners or managers have thought) and action mistakes (the things business owners or managers have done). I hope that breaking these down and providing some context to these mistakes provides some insight for you as a business owner or manager. Perhaps some of these sound familiar, or perhaps they haven't crossed your mind.

THE MOST COMMON DIGITAL MARKETING AND SOCIAL MISTAKES

Out of the countless mistakes that I have witnessed businesses make, the six mistakes I have found to be most frequent in regards to digital marketing and social media are:

Top six thinking mistakes:

- I'm going to get straight into tactics without a clearly defined strategy.

- I can build my own website because programs such as Wix and Squarespace make it easy. I will save myself a tonne of money.

- I can't afford for someone to manage our social media for our business so we will do it in-house.

- I can get someone in [insert foreign country] to do our SEO (search engine optimisation) for one-quarter of the price of getting it done in Australia.

- I can get my friend/brother/sister to design a logo/brochure/ website for me.

- I can do what marketing agencies do myself. Anyone can put ads on Google or Facebook.

Top six action mistakes:

- Jumping straight to tactics; in other words, choosing a path of action (such as SEO, Google AdWords or social media) without knowing or even understanding if the strategy is appropriate and as such whether this is the right tactic.

- Attempting to build a website in-house.

- Wasting time and resources creating poorly conceived content of little value to the intended audience to flood social media, or purchasing "likes" to gain a better "following" on Facebook.

- Engaging a foreign provider for SEO services.

- Engaging a family/friend/amateur to work on their creative material, usually to the detriment of the final outcome.

- Outsourcing Google AdWords or Facebook advertising to foreign countries.

Let's have a closer look at some of these common mistakes.

Jumping straight to tactics

It happens all the time. Business owners come to me and the conversation starts with, "Kevin, we need to do [insert tactic]". There isn't necessarily anything wrong with a conversation starting this way; the issue more so is understanding if this tactic is in fact the most appropriate for this person's objective and the best way in which to attract an audience.

A great example of this was with a potential client I consulted to who operates a unique asset management service for large businesses and government organisations. He was adamant that they needed to be on page one of Google and so required SEO services. I drilled down into that, and this is how the conversation went:

Me: "Why do you need to be on page one of Google?"

Potential client: "Because when you type in [example phrase] we don't come up."

Me: "Why do you need to come up in that search?"

Potential client: "Because … that's what I want to be found for."

Me: "Okay, so tell me a bit about your perfect client. How old are they? How do they behave? Where are they located? What process do they go through to select a similar management service?"

Potential client (I'm paraphrasing here): "They are usually in their mid to late fifties, they are similar to doctors, really time poor, don't tend to consume a lot of media and they typically select similar services through direct communications and responses to tenders."

Me: "So what I'm hearing is that they don't search on Google to find someone to help manage their multi-million-dollar portfolios?"

Potential client: "I guess not … "

Me: "Okay, that's not a problem. Tell me, do you have a database, or have you networked with these potential clients before? Do you know their names perhaps, or where they work, or their job titles?"

Potential client: "Yes, I sure do. I know a lot of the main targets I would like."

Me: "That's great! Here's what I want you to do. Simply write a hand-written letter to each target person on your database. Keep it short and simple. Ask for 20 minutes of their time to discuss their current situation, and their needs and objectives."

Potential client: "Okay ... will do!"

Three weeks later ...

Potential client: "I did what you said Kevin, and I've just been asked to tender for a $250k contract!"

Me: "That's great news! Shall I send you an invoice for 10%?"

Okay, so that last bit was a joke. And sure, I could have charged for a strategy session. But what was literally a 20-minute discussion quickly led me to understand that while the client had an idea of what he felt was the appropriate marketing strategy for him, it actually wasn't. And yes, I could have just agreed, been engaged on a retainer, and begun an SEO strategy, created lots of smart tools and content, but at this point the business really didn't need it, and ethically it would have been remiss of me to suggest otherwise.

The purpose of the above example is to demonstrate that you need to learn how to understand your objectives and your audience so intimately that you are able to ask the right questions, and so avoid either employing the wrong person to drive your marketing strategy or engaging the wrong agency that convinces you to adopt an approach that is simply unnecessary or irrelevant to your customers' purchasing journey.

This is why jumping to tactics is dangerous.

Attempting to build a website in-house

We have had a number of clients who were concerned about the price of a website and have been conditioned to think that all web development is at least somewhat equal. But, interestingly, we have obtained much of our work from clients who have previously engaged sub-par or cheap companies to build their sites who were then burnt when it comes to things such as:

- further development or capability of the site

- management of the back end

- ownership of the domains

- making changes to the site

- the quality of the design

- hosting, customer support and reliability

- poor communication and a misunderstanding of what is required

- the developer withholding access to the files, making it impossible for them to change vendors

- lack of support and strategy in evaluating exactly what the website should contain and how it should be used as a business tool.

They are typically concerned that moving away from this sub-par incumbent could be messy, and they find it difficult to trust that we as an agency will provide a better experience than what they have just been through.

By helping them understand our process, being very transparent about exactly what we offer, and by laying each of the features on the table, they soon come to realise the benefit of engaging strategic marketers to facilitate the build of their website.

We have found that these clients often then double or triple the initial spend on their website as they reach a stage where they understand the further needs and wants of their clients and thus are able to expand their site accordingly and with confidence.

Outsourcing SEO, AdWords or Facebook advertising to a foreign country or amateur/inexperienced provider

Many business owners tend to get somewhat concerned when discussing SEO, AdWords or Facebook advertising. They tend to become overwhelmed and confused (and understandably so) about the variance in price and in service offerings when going to multiple businesses for a quote. The price conscious among them tend to engage an offshore agency (mainly for SEO), as price is a great motivator.

Where they go wrong is that a lack of education and understanding from these suppliers means that they are unaware of the SEO techniques they are implementing, and instead of trying to build a content-rich, informative, authoritative website, these businesses employ "game like" tactics to help the website ranking. What is then discovered is one of two things:

- It becomes unsustainable as the Google algorithm picks up that the traffic coming to the site and the way in which people interact with the site are not genuine and so de-ranks the site; in other words, Google figures out that it is being "tricked" and then pushes the website far down the Google list.

- Google severely penalises the domain by blacklisting it. This means it basically shuts the site down or stops "crawling" it (which means that Google basically ignores it and lists it as an inappropriate site). Recovery from this is very difficult, often requiring you to start from scratch.

As you can see, this can be a very costly mistake to make.

We have seen a number of clients come to us after going down this path. They often trial us for a three- to six-month period in order to ascertain the value, the service and the metrics-driven yield on their investment. All of our clients who partake in SEO, AdWords or Facebook Ads have retained us on an ongoing basis for a number of years, because they learn the value of implementing these systems properly. We also get to a point in the relationship whereby if the campaigns are not yielding the results the customer would have anticipated then we will gladly cease a campaign in the best interests of the client.

Purchasing "likes" to gain a larger following on Facebook

Some business owners tend to believe that "a 'like' is a 'like'" on Facebook. But not all "likes" are created equal. The "buying" of "likes" to build a following is a trend that Facebook is working hard to stamp out. There are services out there that use bots and fake accounts to drive the "likes" of a Facebook page up. For example, each of these "likes" may cost $0.05 to $0.20 each.

When these "likes" are purchased, Facebook eventually catches on to the fake accounts and will shut them down. And those that manage to fly under the radar and remain active will be effectively worthless as they are not a qualified or valuable audience that you can market to or use to leverage for further marketing activities or promotion. When you understand the differences between buying "likes" and building solid, quantitative campaigns that will yield a focused and dedicated audience, you will realise that buying "likes" is not an effective strategy, merely a short-term fix.

A genuinely interested Facebook audience is a valuable asset for your business. You will have an audience that engages with you, is qualified (that is, has been targeted and meets your criteria for demographic, geographic and psychographic), and is actively interested in your products and services.

The analogy I like to use here is: would you rather be in a room with 50 people who are massively and genuinely interested in everything you have to say, hanging off each word? Or would you rather be in front of 50,000 people but only 50 of those people are genuinely interested in what you have to say?

I know where I'd rather be.

Attempting to manage social media in-house

Often small business owners do not see the immediate value in building a strong and engaged social network for their business. The suggestion of engaging a specialist agency to conduct this work either on their behalf or in conjunction with them through an investment challenges these thoughts even further.

Because social media is usually a "free" platform, the average user feels a sense of confidence in managing their social media in-house and treating it very similarly to their own personal account. What tends to go wrong here is that without a formal strategy, a plan for the curation of content and in-depth understanding of their target audience or the mechanics of successful social posting, the value behind the channel is quickly diminished. The audience doesn't engage with the brand, their posting frequency is inconsistent and content is not always relevant, and this often "turns off" the audience.

A good marketing agency will provide ultimate customer and audience value. They will take care of the important content, the regular posting, the key content strategies, and the audience appeal. They will guide the clients with their posting and their content curation at a "front line level" in order to give the brand more personality.

Once the social channel starts yielding dialogue and engagement, and is used for enquiries, sales and customer service, the business owner tends to adopt a more focused and active approach to their social channels. We have witnessed clients spending 50% to 80% of their marketing dollars purely on social media for this very reason.

Engaging a family/friend/amateur to work on creative content

Engaging someone on a free, contract or low-cost arrangement is understandable when starting out in business. Logos, branding, collateral and design overall has been somewhat commoditised. But what tends to go wrong is there's a lack of understanding of the importance of the brand, and what that means when conducting business, and also growing it.

For example, I have seen business owners create brands that are aimed at being developed into franchises or multi-location businesses. What often gets overlooked are the implications of an "off the shelf" logo, such as breaching copyright, not using unique fonts, wanting to trademark it down the track, and so on.

Once a business owner understands the long-term needs of the business, and has a vision of where they want to take their business and the way in which their audience will respond to their brand, they quickly begin to see the value a focused brand development strategy and creative approach can have. And the only way to achieve this is using marketing and design professionals. So, what may seem like a cost saving at the outset can be to the long-term detriment of the business.

Businesses owners who make the required investment to do this properly upfront are grateful that the brand they have invested in stands the test of time. They don't consider rebranding, and they value the guidance placed on the brand as a component of their IP.

A CHECKPOINT

The takeaway from this chapter should be an intention to understand where businesses tend to go wrong, and for you to be able to relate to these issues in a way that helps you avoid the many mistakes and pitfalls lots of other business owners have made. Whether you choose to engage professionals in-house to provide this service to you, or alternatively seek to outsource to a professional organisation to support these efforts, qualify them with the above information and ensure they too don't employ (or intend to employ) these tactics.

As a business owner or manager, try to make a point of valuing your marketing, digital platforms and social media as important assets to your business. Using the notes section as a checkpoint in the book, ask yourself:

- Have you ever made any of the mistakes in this chapter? If so, what did you learn?

- Do you now value the importance of having a sound and considered strategy relating to your digital marketing and social media approach?

- Do you value the importance of engaging the right expertise for the development and execution of your main digital and social deliverables?

- Do you understand the detriments of engaging amateurs?

NOTES:

NOTES:

4

THE TRUTH? YOU CAN'T HANDLE THE TRUTH! (OR CAN YOU?)

Clients, ambitious clients, from established businesses, that are hungry, that are willing to do what it takes to get the best results possible for their business are the ones I love working with the most.

The reason I (and my team) love working with them the most is that they have been around long enough to have learned from their mistakes. They value people's time, their energy and their expertise. They tend to understand that they "can't do it all themselves". They are insightful enough to understand that marketing has changed, and they understand that the definition of insanity is "doing the same thing over and over again, yet expecting a different result".

In my initial meeting with potential clients, I usually say this: "I won't piss in your pocket and I don't stroke egos. You are either going to appreciate and respect me for my professional opinion, and the fact that I call a spade a spade, or you are not. And if not, I completely respect that and I will gladly shake hands and we can go our separate ways." This usually helps identify those who are genuinely willing to learn and work with us, rather than those who are more concerned with their image than their results.

The reason I believe this is so important is because of one simple thing: the truth. That's right, the truth.

Sounds simple, doesn't it? Sadly, it doesn't seem to be. Let's find out why.

CHOOSING THE RIGHT AGENCY FOR YOUR BUSINESS

We (marketers) work in an industry with "low barriers to entry". This means someone could literally wake up one morning, decide they are going to be a "marketing/digital/social media consultant", and go out there and start selling their services to businesses. Sure, most businesses will likely have a way of sounding them out. They often ask for a portfolio, experience, and anecdotes about things this person has achieved, yet it amazes me the number of people out there who have used Facebook for a whole five seconds who are claiming to be social media experts, or the person who "built" a Wix site once and thinks they are a developer.

Okay, perhaps I am exaggerating a bit, but here's the point: it pains me because I studied both undergraduate and post graduate qualifications over a 14-year period in marketing and business management, right up to a Master of Business Administration (MBA, majoring in Marketing). To be honest, the educational component for me as I see it was really just a series of tools which helped me establish a level of critical and strategic thinking that helps serve as a foundation for a lot of what we do, yet what is most valuable is the way that education has translated through experience in my career. I have lived and breathed this for the last 16 years.

The industry doesn't have a compliance requirement like accountants or lawyers do. We don't have to study for seven years and be qualified like a doctor does before we can advise a company on their strategy. What we do have to do however is get results.

We need to invest in ourselves first, and ensure we are keeping up to date with the technology, the changes, the platforms, the methods, and the mediums to deliver a great digital marketing and social media experience. The last six years of my career in particular have seen me invest almost two hours a day into my education, reading the content put out there by the leading platforms, keeping up to date with the latest development trends, changes in algorithms, understanding the user experience, marketing techniques, and engaging the experts who have learned to specialise in each of the marketing channels.

In an industry that is basically unregulated, as business owners you want to ensure that your digital marketing and social media experts are accountable for delivering the overall objectives you have set out to achieve. You should demand the truth from the experts you speak with.

THE TRUTH ABOUT THE AGENCY

I believe that many business owners have been seduced by the prospect of digital marketing and social media, as it has often been depicted as a magic bullet, the misconception of a single-pronged approach that will solve all of your troubles, building you an unbelievably loyal audience and yielding incredible returns. Frankly, this isn't always the case. Be wary of whom you choose to engage, ask for evidence for what they tell you, and for genuine testimonials. Ask them where they have failed, and where they have succeeded. Ask them about the clients they have won and the clients they have lost, and ask them why.

Listen for the cues, the cues that show how they have taken ownership of their failures, where they have honestly put their hand on their heart and realised that they couldn't get the results they had anticipated, or where a client has grown out of them and moved onto the next level, or where they've simply made a mistake. This is truth. There is no such thing as a perfect digital marketing and social media agency. We can't predict the future, but we can do everything humanly possible to ensure we are putting our best foot forward, using experience and qualified data, conducting research, and learning about and understanding a market and a target audience to maximise every opportunity and yield the best results.

THE TRUTH ABOUT YOUR BUSINESS

Here's the last piece of cold, hard honesty. And it's about your business. If your product or service offering is misaligned with your customers' expectations, if your customer experience falls short, if the claims you make that entice people to transact with you are not delivered, if you don't stand by what you deliver, or the offers you provide are uncompetitive, then no amount of marketing is going to help you. Simply be honest in your engagement with your customers and we all reap the benefits.

So let's make sure we all get it right.

A CHECKPOINT

Use the notes here as a checkpoint to review the following:

- Have you used an agency in the past? If so, what did you learn from the experience? If not, why not?

- If you were planning to engage an agency, what would you look for?

- If you were interviewing an agency, what are the questions you would ask and what is most important to you and your business?

NOTES:

NOTES:

5

UNDERSTANDING THE UNIVERSAL LANGUAGE OF MARKETING

WHAT *IS* MARKETING?

The definition of marketing published by the UK's Chartered Institute of Marketing is "the management process responsible for identifying, anticipating and satisfying customer needs profitably". I think that's pretty spot on. Whether you are a business that does all of your marketing in-house, or you outsource portions or the whole function to an agency, that is what marketing as a function is tasked to do.

WHO ARE YOU SELLING TO?

The process of identifying, anticipating and satisfying customers' needs in a profitable way is the same regardless of industry. Every business has customers but some are called clients; some are called consumers and some are other businesses.

In the marketing world, this is traditionally broken down as follows:

- **B2B – business to business:** This is where businesses sell and transact with other businesses. They might have enterprise products, or provide professional services to businesses, and not a general "consumer".

- **B2C – business to consumer:** This is where businesses specifically target the general consumer. They will be very focused on their target audience; the aim here is to pick a specific mix (for example, men, aged 25 to 35, who play a particular sport, live in the inner west and earn over $80,000 per annum) and market to that specific demographic.

Without overcomplicating things, the primary difference between marketing to a business and marketing to a consumer tends to sit in the tactics. As you can imagine, you have different audiences that need to be "touched" in different ways, at different times, and through potentially different channels. (In marketing we call every interaction with a brand, business, service or product a "touch".)

However, I believe that there is no longer a definitive division required between the B2B approach and the B2C approach in the traditional sense. As business owners or managers, if you are traditionally marketing or selling to other businesses (as opposed to a "consumer" or end user), you must understand that these businesses are made up of individuals – it is *people* we sell and market to, not "entities". An entity is just a piece of paper. This traditional approach to segmenting an audience is now largely redundant as digital and social channels are more focused on individual behaviours, and on tapping into those behaviours to position a product or service accordingly.

We could call this **P2P – people to people** or **person to person** – marketing, whereby personal messages are created in a way that relates to other people; that is, individuals who can relate to the content and the underlying messages. Even if purchasing decisions are made by boards or panels where there are multiple decision makers involved in the process, the same applies – our role as strategic marketers is still to understand each of the people involved in the decision-making process and how to leverage digital and social channels best to aid how you and your business communicates with them. We touch on this more in the social and digital media section.

MARKETING TRANSCENDS INDUSTRIES
What I love about marketing is how it translates across so many countries, cultures, industries and generations. The universal language of marketing that I refer to is that of your digital marketing and social media approach, and how similar strategies can translate across multiple industries.

Many businesses are concerned that without an intimate knowledge of their product, service or industry it can be difficult for marketers to really understand how to market the business. I challenge this view. I challenge this view because I believe it is our job as marketers to use the tools, techniques, strategies and research to help make strategic decisions, and these methods can be applied to just about any industry. Don't get me wrong: I am not talking about a "cookie-cutter" approach, more so an understanding that the primary value is in what we are trained to learn and understand quickly in order to make strategic decisions.

Further, and most importantly, I believe our job as marketers is to gain an intimate understanding and knowledge of our audience. Even if you are doing this in-house and are working out who is the ultimate customer for your product or service, your goal as a business owner or manager is to know everything about them.

PROFILING METHODOLOGY

Everything we should do from a strategic marketing standpoint comes back to something known as a "profiling methodology", which is the way in which we tend to break down an audience. It is as simple as:

- **Demographics:** age, sex, nationality, ethnicity, religion.
- **Socioeconomic:** income, job status/level, education, wealth, location.
- **Psychographic:** options, thoughts, values, morals, interests, attitudes.
- **Geographic:** physical location, where they live, where they visit, where they travel to, where they came from, where they went.

Once you become familiar with all of this information you have the ability to determine the best approach to your digital marketing and social media needs. The behaviours and profile of your customer are critical in ascertaining the best strategies. Understanding these also ensures that you enlist the best approach that will avoid wasting money.

A great example of not understanding this, which you may well have seen in your local area, is obstetricians advertising on the sides of busses. This is what we call an "above the line" marketing technique. It's basically a mass market strategy. As you could imagine, there is a *huge* amount of waste involved in the process. While I am certain that expectant mothers would see this ad, the rest of the population will see it too. What this means is that the message is only relevant to a small percentage of the population. What's more, in my opinion it's an irrelevant marketing exercise – that money could be invested in truly valuable marketing strategies aimed at expectant or planning-to-be mothers and fathers, and engaging them in a more personal and meaningful way.

If we think about how this audience behaves, you could be certain that they are searching online for information about the birth of their child, or what to consider when planning a family (in fact Google has tools that allow you to see the volume of searches that are done every day for any given keyword or phrase). You could also be sure they are asking other mothers who have been through the process. They are likely to join Facebook groups and communities, they will research or purchase particular books, follow particular experts, and they are likely to speak to their GP.

So, given the information above, do you see any value in an obstetrician advertising on a bus? What is the call to action? Would you expect that someone would call to enquire about the obstetrician on the side of the bus? In marketing terms, the only reason for this form of advertising is brand awareness as a touch point. It is ensuring that the obstetrician is seen as being personable, local and of scale (the perception is that major advertisements indicate that a company is quite large). But this is a very expensive way to achieve these outcomes.

You might also notice a similar strategy being implemented by your local real estate agents, on bus shelters and billboards. The aim is to create a level of familiarity and personality so that when you come to buying or selling a home and you meet the agents, they seem somewhat relatable.

What I love the most about all things digital marketing and social media is that the methods translate across industries. The following chapters explore how digital marketing and social media can work regardless of the industry you are in.

A CHECKPOINT

Use this as a checkpoint to think about your PERFECT customer. Have a go at profiling them using the profiling methodology. Be as detailed as you possibly can.

NOTES:

PART II

UNDERSTANDING DIGITAL MARKETING AND SOCIAL MEDIA OBJECTIVES FOR YOUR BUSINESS

6

IT'S MORE THAN
JUST SALES

THAT WAS THEN

Jeffrey Gitomer, author and sales expert, said, "People don't like to be sold, but they love to buy". Sales is sales, marketing is marketing. Well, traditionally they were. These two areas used to be very distinct roles and operations, which operated hand in hand and were complementary to each other. If you just want to "sell" then you may not even need marketing (sure, you can get a glossy brochure with features and benefits on it made and call that "marketing"). You can go door to door, or get a stall at the markets or a shopping centre, and let your product or service do the talking.

But what happens when there are 5, 10, 15 competitors selling the same thing you are? What is the compelling reason someone would buy from *you*? How would they hear about you in the first place? How do they know that you should be chosen?

THIS IS NOW

With so many channels to market these days, and the way in which communication has become a two-way dialogue rather than a one-way "push", the line between sales and marketing has been blurred; in fact, you could argue it doesn't exist anymore.

The advent of social media, and the creation of meaningful, educational, informative, insightful and engaging content, has challenged the traditional approach. No longer are we just throwing a brand out into the market hoping for the best, or producing some marketing collateral to complement the sales pitch. What we are doing now is creating meaningful relationships with our audience. We are telling stories, taking people on a journey, educating them, showing them the "human" element to our business, promoting individuals, and highlighting the contributions the business is making to society as a whole.

IS MARKETING RESPONSIBLE FOR SALES?

So the Question could be asked: *is marketing responsible for sales?*

Before we answer this, consider again the definition of marketing we used in chapter 5 from the UK's Chartered Institute of Marketing: "the management process responsible for identifying, anticipating and satisfying customer needs profitably".

In other words, the marketing function plays a role far greater than just doing "the sell". Marketing plays a critical role in achieving two key things: brand awareness and lead generation. When these two components combine, and your target audience enters your space, you have the ability to take them on a journey to sale whereby the transaction simply becomes a formality.

THE KEY OBJECTIVES

What has this all got to do with objectives then? Well, the important takeaway here is that when setting your objectives for your marketing or social media efforts, setting one such as "I just want more sales" is not going to solve the problem. Sure, you might hit some short-term goals, but where is the sustainability? How do you keep your customers or clients coming back? How can you ensure that you are referred or reviewed positively?

And herein lies the key to setting your objectives: understanding that each of your efforts should set out to achieve a number of goals, with the ultimate objective being not only a sale but a customer experience that leaves them begging for more and keeps them coming back time and time again.

The following chapters explore the key objectives primarily used in the digital space, albeit they can translate to traditional methods as well. These are:

- brand awareness
- lead generation
- engagement and community
- traffic.

PAID, OWNED, EARNED

So why is understanding these objectives so important? *Paid, owned, earned* is why.

You may have heard these terms before. Marketers have a tendency to use them all the time, primarily because it helps cement the importance of the digital and social marketing mix you employ, and why they all come together (see the Venn diagram on the following page).

Paid

I've said it before – we have been given so many great "free" channels that allow us to interact with our audience; however, just like traditional media, if we wish to amplify this and reach and engage more, we have to invest. In essence, this is simply advertising. It could be pay per click, Facebook or other social media ads, remarketing and retargeting, paying influencers, or paying for content development. The purpose of this is known as "outreach", which is a simple way of saying that you use paid methods to seed and amplify your content and channels.

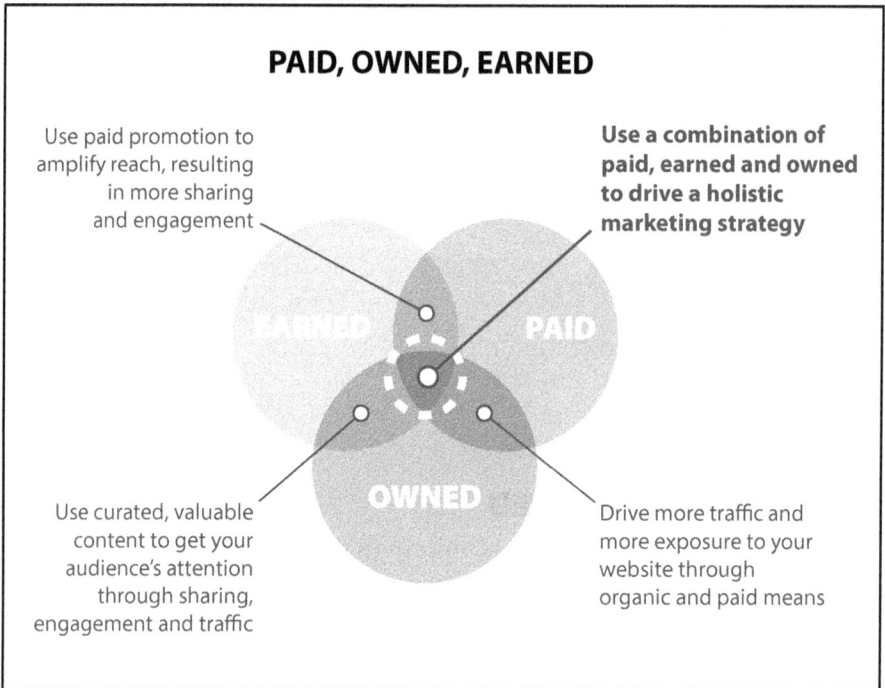

PAID, OWNED, EARNED

Use paid promotion to amplify reach, resulting in more sharing and engagement

Use a combination of paid, earned and owned to drive a holistic marketing strategy

EARNED

PAID

OWNED

Use curated, valuable content to get your audience's attention through sharing, engagement and traffic

Drive more traffic and more exposure to your website through organic and paid means

Owned

Each of your channels that you own is valuable to you and your business. You own that form of media, you control the communications, and can set the tone for dialogue. These sources include your social media channels, your website, your blog and any other channel that you have complete control over.

Earned

This is where valuable content becomes so important, because while you can pay to get your content out there, if the content is no good or lacks quality or relevance then you are wasting your time. *Earned* exposure is the objective, and is represented by the number of people who engage with your content, who share your content, who comment on your content, and provide reviews on your business.

* * * * *

What is important to note is that objectives tend not to be set in isolation but in combination. Good campaigns have goals for a number of objectives, with measures in place for each. Keep this in mind when reading the following chapters.

> *What is important to note is that objectives tend not to be set in isolation but in combination.*

A CHECKPOINT

Use the notes to think about what objectives you believe your business may need. Jot down some ideas about how your paid, owned and earned channels could be improved.

NOTES:

7

UNDERSTANDING BRAND AWARENESS

THE DIFFICULTIES OF MEASURING BRAND AWARENESS

If there is one thing that used to really irk me back in the day of my employed marketing career, it was the use of the term "brand awareness" to justify a Marketing Manager's position. So many agencies would try to sell the term "brand awareness" to justify the spend of a campaign. It was a matter of simply putting the brand out there and their job was done, and there could be tens, if not hundreds of thousands – or even millions – of dollars dedicated to it.

The difficulty with brand awareness is that the only way you can genuinely measure the effectiveness of a campaign is to interview a large enough sample size of your target audience, and ask them (unprompted) about the brands they relate to (either the products or services). Further, this is then correlated with prompted questions about brands (where the person being surveyed is exposed to a series of brands, one of which would be the brand being measured), and they would then share which of these they knew about, as well as what the brand actually does (being aware of the brand is one thing, but knowing what the brand is or does is another).

I am simplifying things here, but this kind of research, done properly, is typically quite expensive. In my corporate days working for a global leader in industrial products and heading up the marketing function in Australia, we did just that. I recall a low six-figure price tag to conduct the research (and that was at the cheaper end of the equation), which was both qualitative and quantitative. Over 1000 businesses in our target market were interviewed, across the country, with the sample size being split to reflect the size of each market in each state, at a 98% confidence level. The data was incredible: it allowed us to evaluate where we stood in the market, compared to where we had come from; it allowed us to determine if we would be selected for purchasing, or if we were just one in the mix when it came to purchasing; and ultimately it gave us a huge insight into our business and the market, and allowed us to establish 10 key areas in which we could make strategic decisions.

Please don't get me wrong. I am not saying there isn't a place for brand awareness. In fact, it still should play a pivotal role in your marketing strategy, regardless of whether you are selling direct to consumers or are selling to individuals within businesses. Ultimately your target audience needs to be aware of you. The challenge though for most businesses I work with is that even the largest of organisations ($500m+) typically don't have the budget to put that much money towards evaluating their brand awareness. They are usually investing their marketing dollars in strategies that yield clear growth.

What is important is the way in which you go about generating and ultimately measuring that brand awareness. Setting brand awareness as a strategy in isolation is old hat. As mentioned above, just sticking an ad out there no longer has a place on its own. What is important are the channels you select, the messages that you put out there, and their intention and required action.

TODAY, CONTENT IS KING

This ultimately revolves around content. You may well have heard the phrase "content is king", and it's absolutely correct. This is nothing new, however the advent of multiple digital marketing channels has multiplied the importance of creating valuable content.

Imagine this.

You know exactly who your target audience is. You know everything about their profile, how they behave, what they do, what they think, their age, location, and so on. But they don't know about you. You want them to know about you but you're unsure about how to best do that. This is where brand awareness through valuable content comes in.

Your audience, regardless of who they are, would have questions relating to your product or service, yet they don't necessarily know that your product or service is the solution to their problem. For example, a consumer might know they are thirsty, yet when they go into the shop to buy a drink, they may not know what they are thirsty for. Likewise, a senior manager within a business might be thinking about a better way to manage their contacts, yet isn't necessarily sure what the best method or program would be to organise this information.

So think about this. Imagine if you could help your audience by providing regular information (content) to them which answers the questions they have. It doesn't even necessarily have to be exactly aligned with what you do, but there will be a correlation between the two. To some (and I have had these conversations) it sounds like an odd concept that you would provide educational information to your target audience that isn't necessarily "selling" your product or service. What it does do, however, is position you within your target audience as a product or service provider that understands their needs and answers their questions.

Providing value to your audience

Here's a great example. We have worked with a client who supplies Australia's leading product for keeping leaves out of gutters and is endorsed by a famous ex-cricketer and Australian icon. It is the leading product in the marketplace for a number of reasons.

Most people would be aware that leaves in their gutter are a problem, yet they may be unaware of the best solution to stop this, and further what the best or most suitable product would be.

The typical marketing approach in this situation for a business is to ensure you are creating a very clear point of difference as to why yours is the leading product, and why a customer would pay a premium for it. Usually you go down the "features" and "benefits" path. However, most of the content we have created in this case is not about keeping leaves out of the gutter but about telling the stories that relate to the customers and the issues, concerns or pain they are having. We would write articles about the best ways in which to maintain a garden (to stop the leaves becoming a problem in the first place), we would write about ways in which to reduce fire hazards on your property, or we would talk about seasonal maintenance programs. All these articles would be of value and interest and engage the target audience.

Interestingly, while working with this company we also discovered something else aside from the content value we can create for their normal audience: we discovered that there are a huge number of people who have problems with possums in their roof, and they are unsure of the best way to keep them out. As such, when thinking laterally about this, we created specific content about the ways to keep possums out of gutters. We created some really powerful graphics, and disseminated that information into the marketplace. Of course, it was branded with the client's logo, and the information led people back to their website to read about this. While this information wasn't specifically about the client's product (keeping leaves out of the gutter), what this did was create immense value and solved an audience's problem (keeping possums out of the gutter and from getting into the roof cavity). Ultimately our research showed that the audience and the market had questions that needed to be answered, which we were aware of because we knew the audience well (how they behaved and what their problems were), and we answered those questions in a simple, interesting and engaging way.

Another great example of building brand awareness through content development with the objective to drive action was a campaign we executed for the leading tow bar manufacturer in Australia. The need we wanted to address was the importance of weighing your caravan, boat, horse trailer or any other item you plan to tow. The purpose of this exercise is to first establish if a weight distribution system is required, and secondly to explain the impact weight distribution has in towing these heavy items. What we demonstrated was the need to educate our audience and provide them with valuable information (in this case written content and video), via a dedicated landing page which took users on a journey, helping them understand in a clear and concise manner the importance of this subject. The results were nothing short of stellar: a 97% increase in quotes generated for the product from a single content-based campaign.

Get the picture?

I believe this is a great example of how brand awareness for most businesses can be created and the impact measured. The impact can be measured by the response to the content you put out. How many people saw it? How many people engaged with it? How many people acted on it? How many people shared it around? And so on.

Sure, I get that the major difference here (in comparison to dedicated marketing research) is that there isn't a sound measure for aware versus unaware, or prompted versus unprompted, but as far as I am concerned, this is just as valuable, if not more so. Ultimately, a quality piece of content has been created to drive an unaware market to a possible solution for their problem. Further, this content can be clearly tracked every step of the way (the joys of the digital world), and has the ability to drive interest and ultimately conversion.

The takeaway from all of this is that it is okay to set brand awareness as one of your marketing objectives, but set it in such a way that allows you to be valuable to an audience and ultimately your customers. Do it in such a way that can be tracked, that allows you to evaluate the effectiveness of what you put out there.

Foster a business culture that elevates the "success" of a campaign beyond "eyeballs" or "impressions". (Impressions are the number of times your brand, content, page or advertisement has been shown or displayed on various mediums. For example, a display banner on a website might have received 10,000 impressions.) Our aim in marketing is to tie back the objectives to something that is tangible, where we can qualify the results and be sure that what we have put out there is relevant, engaging, and has been given the time and attention it deserves, while ultimately driving a response or action.

CONTENT CLARIFIED

So you've heard the word "content". You're exposed to it daily, you know it's typically an important component of a sound marketing strategy: but what exactly is it? Is it video? Is it pictures? Is it a blog? Put simply, it's all of the above, and more.

Content allows you to provide value to your audience *before* you "sell" to them; in other words, you can educate, inform and engage them. So what kinds of content are there, you ask?

Here's some of the most common forms of content:

- **Articles:** these could be about your business, your product or your services. Include information that is topical, timely and relevant.

- **Aggregators:** this is when you create either a landing page or content page on your website which brings together a whole lot of information that is valuable to your customers, and either displays the various information or links to them.

- **Calendars:** you could create brand, product or service related calendars for your customers.

- **Checklists:** this could be a checklist of things they need, things they should consider or things you want or need them to do.

- **Ebooks:** you can do this if you've written a book, or you can create a book-style piece of content that can be shared digitally.

- **Expert tips:** be the expert or engage one to come up with tips, ideas or suggestions relevant to your audience.

- **Glossary:** explain the language of your industry in simple language, so your audience can understand what's going on.

- **How to:** teach your audience something useful with a "how to" guide.

- **In-depth guides:** get more detailed and provide a comprehensive training program or step-by-step manual.

- **Infographics:** combine information and graphics to communicate data or information.

- **Interviews:** speak to experts or to existing customers and capture it on video or audio.

- **Listicles:** these are like articles but instead of writing paragraphs you write a bullet point list and expand on each bullet.

- **Memes/gifs:** you've seen them – they can be funny, educational or informative.

- **News:** like an article but relevant to your business or industry and of interest to your audience.

- **PDF downloads:** these can be any of the content pieces that you have created in a static or graphic format.

- **Podcasts:** a little more involved, typically including discussing questions, subjects or topics that relate to and resonate with your audience.

- **Product reviews:** these can be video or graphically created, where you provide an overview of a product and your experience with it.

- **Recipes:** these don't need to be cooking related; you might have a five-step process in your business – why not turn those steps into a "recipe"?

- **Research papers:** great for industries where data and research are fundamental in building authority and educating an audience.

- **Tables:** a simple way of displaying information.

- **Timelines:** used to convey a message or events that happen over a period of time. For example, it could be showing the steps over time in achieving a goal that your business offers its customers, or the steps in building, creating, or manufacturing a particular outcome.

- **Transcriptions:** this is where you might conduct an interview, or record answers to questions, then get it professionally transcribed and turned into a blog, article or news piece.

- **Tutorial videos:** a great tool if your product or service is involved and people would value guidance to either get the most out of it or learn about it and how to use it, either pre or post purchase. Further, this could also be educational content that teaches your audience how to do particular things.

What's important to note here (and *this* is the key) is that this content doesn't always need to be about you, your business, your brand, or your service or product (gasp! shock horror! how can that be?).

That's right. It's *not* about you.

It's about your *audience*. Why do we forget these people? You know, the ones who pay our bills, the ones that we want to walk through our door, or call our number? Okay, I am being facetious, however there's a tendency to think that if you're going to create this content, it may as well be about your business. Wrong. Make it about your audience – if you put yourself in the shoes of your customer, what do *they* really want? For example, when you buy a drill bit, do you really want the drill bit, or do you want the hole it creates? If you buy an air conditioner, do you want the unit itself or do you want cool or warm air in your house? You buy the result and you buy the outcome; the physical product or service is a means to an end.

The same applies to content production. Audiences want content and information that's relevant to them, that appeals to them because it might answer their questions, or provide interesting or informative ways to solve a problem they have, or perhaps they need to learn more about a brand, product or service, so do it in a way that talks about what matters to them (that is, the outcomes or results they should expect). Think of creating content that behaves like that friend you know and trust at a dinner party who provides some great insight, advice or information that really resonates with you on a particular topic. Don't be that infomercial telling you to "buy now", "get in fast" or "call now for a free set of steak knives".

A CHECKPOINT
Why not use this point in the book to come up with 5 to 10 brand awareness/content pieces you could create that would be of interest or value to your target audience?

NOTES:

NOTES:

8

UNDERSTANDING
LEAD GENERATION

For many businesses, a strong marketing machine does this function really well. It's a simple concept: create a marketing strategy that is designed to drive a steady flow of leads which meet a predetermined criterion. The more focused the campaign, the better your targeting, and the sharper your communications are with your ideal audience, the better quality the leads will be.

The purpose of lead generation is also very deliberate. This is typically where your audience enters their interaction with you; they may have seen something, or heard something, or perhaps were looking for something and didn't know where to start.

When we talk about lead generation in this book, I am generally referring to digital lead generation as opposed to analogue leads (that is, someone completing a paper form, obtaining businesses cards, and so on), simply because the majority of interactions taking place today are digital.

Leads come in many different forms. Some simple examples of leads are:

- a full name

- an email address

- a phone number

- a survey response.

SOWING THE RIGHT SEEDS

These leads are extremely valuable if harvested correctly. The term "harvested" is fitting. I believe that leads need to be nurtured – good leads, that is … quality leads that will turn into valuable customers.

Seeds are sown in the right environment. Those seeds are tended to, watered, given sun and fertiliser, are kept free from bugs and threats, and are given the chance to grow. Once fully grown, they are harvested to then be processed, packaged, sold and consumed.

The process for lead generation is very much the same. You can plant a seed with valuable content (see chapter 7 and the way in which I explore brand awareness in relation to content creation), and nurture that content through the right channels. The popularity of and interest in your content then grows as your audience grows. The interest from that audience then grows into a lead (someone who takes action and parts with something, even if it's just time or information). This is what you then harvest to take them to next stages (engagement, interaction, information, education, parting with more time, sales, and so on).

All too often when we engage with clients their initial thoughts are that they want to reach everyone their product or service is relevant to. I've worked with accountants who want to target *anyone* who files a tax return, I've worked with removalists who want to target *everyone* who wants to move interstate, and I've worked with e-tailers who want to target *anyone* with a car. This is great if you have an unlimited budget, but most established businesses have allocated a set percentage of their revenue towards their marketing, and they expect to make a measurable return on this investment.

Whenever I am faced with such requests, I bring the client back to these two questions:

- Who or what is your ideal client? (This is where the profiling methodology comes in; see chapter 5.)

- What product or service yields you the greatest profit?

These two questions alone typically allow us to develop a strong lead generation campaign that is laser focused on a very specific group of people (the target audience) and on driving interest towards a product that is highly profitable for the client. The ultimate result here is a steady flow of interest that is aimed at:

- converting a high-profit product or service

- creating a strong platform for business growth

- building an authentic and qualified user base or database for further development and interaction

- enabling the profit to allow for reinvestment into generating new campaigns and targeting different segments or audiences.

HIGHLY QUALIFIED AND TARGETED LEADS

An important thing to understand in the digital marketing space is what it takes to generate a lead. Generating a highly qualified and targeted lead requires a laser focus on that particular objective.

To be effective with your lead generation campaigns, I believe you need to have an understanding of the process that goes behind the generation of leads online. The reason this is valuable is that placing a single ad on Facebook or Google is unlikely to yield the results you are after.

Let's face it, you are reading this book because you just want it to work, so here it is – a basic guide to setting up and implementing a lead generation campaign:

1   **Audience:** Know who your audience is, including all of their demographic, socioeconomic, psychographic and geographic information (see "profiling methodology" in chapter 5).

2   **Product/service:** Understand the specific product or service that is most relevant to your audience, and ensure that it yields profitable returns when you convert.

3   **Content:** Develop interesting, engaging, educational and informative content that addresses particular questions your potential customers might have or potentially solves current problems they are searching for answers to.

4   **Channel:** Fish where the fish are. Sounds obvious, but this is often overlooked. Some basic research will help you identify the places your audience frequents:

- Are they on Facebook? (It's very likely they are.)

- Do they search using Google? (They probably do, but what are they searching for?)

- What websites do they visit? (Are they on eBay and Gumtree? Or do they read the *Australian Financial Review* every day?)

- Are they regularly on mobile devices or in front of a computer?

5   **Campaign:** What words would appeal to them? What images resonate with your audience? You have around a one- to two-second window to capture their attention; what is so compelling about your content and why should they click on your ad?

6   **Budget:** Set a number you are comfortable with. Just like your personal spending, avoid spending beyond your means. Always take a conservative approach to begin with. (We touch on this more in part III.)

7   **Monitor, test, optimise, refine:** Monitoring is the key to success when executing digital campaigns. It is important that you carefully watch and analyse what is happening. Are you getting an immediate response? Or are people seeing the campaign but not acting? Testing is also important; in the marketing world, one option is "A/B split testing", which is a fancy way of saying that we will use, say, five different images in a campaign, or five different sets of straplines or hooks, with different image combinations, to see which piece of content generates the best response. Then we cull the baddies, optimise where we can, and push the good ones harder.

HANDY THINGS TO KNOW

Here's a few handy things to know, whether you choose to do this yourself or you engage an agency to execute a campaign for you:

- In my experience it takes on average 8 to 12 "touches" before someone takes action. What this means is that your audience may need to see a message across different channels (on average across 4) between 8 to 12 times before they choose to engage with it or act.

- The key to ensuring your audience is touched multiple times is through a digital strategy called retargeting or remarketing. In principle they do the same thing: they capture your audience's behaviour and respond accordingly. For example, a person has clicked on an ad or visited a website. The digital platforms capture that information, and when that person is perusing other websites or scrolling through Facebook, for example, they will be shown more ads related to where they clicked or visited. (Sound familiar? Now that you are aware of it, you will notice it all the time.) Retargeting is the process whereby you take that audience who has acted in some way and continue to show them your advertisement. Remarketing is typically related to ecommerce, where the potential customer views a product or abandons a shopping cart and then your ad continues to display that product to that person, or even offers a discount on that product. Effectively this strategy ensures that your target audience is seeing your ad, your message or your content numerous times to increase the chances that they act. Both Facebook and Google have this function; it requires a special string of code (called a "pixel") to be inserted into your website code to allow Facebook or Google to track your audience's behaviour once they have visited your site, or clicked on various pages.

- Once your audience has been touched with a particular piece of content on average around 12 times (subject to what the data is telling you), that may be the point where you see a campaign begin to stagnate as the content doesn't "cut through" any more. This is the point where you may evaluate or change the content or campaign objective.

If lead generation is one of your objectives, the underlying premise to all of this is that you have carefully considered the entire process and you are armed with the best available knowledge to make great decisions. All too often we see businesses lured by a "Boost Your Post for only $27" ad on Facebook or "Create your first Google AdWords account and get a $150 cash bonus". This is simply not a productive approach. There is no quick fix and no short cuts. Without an adequate understanding of your market and your audience, and the way in which they behave, and without giving them something of value by way of content, it's fair to say you may as well just throw your money down the drain, as the results simply won't be there.

A CHECKPOINT

Use the notes section and the basic guide to setting up and implementing a lead generation campaign to draft up the basis of a campaign. This could be used later to execute internally or to provide a brief to a third-party agency.

NOTES:

9

UNDERSTANDING ENGAGEMENT AND COMMUNITY

Let me start by saying that when we speak of engagement and community, we are referring to *digital* engagement and *digital* community. This translates into a physical opportunity of course, however the foundations are all set online through digital and social media channels, with the aim of driving physical engagement (contact, traffic, phone calls, sales, and so on).

COMMUNICATION IS NO LONGER ONE WAY

Many people would be aware of or at least understand the basic premise of social media. While they may not understand the difference between Twitter and Facebook, or Snapchat and Instagram, they would generally understand that social media platforms enable the creation of social dialogue and social sharing on a large, borderless scale.

No longer is communication from businesses one way. Traditional marketing focused purely on "push strategies", whereby companies would repetitively put out messages through a number of different channels, with the aim of enticing action; hence radio, television, print and billboards were so popular. Of course, for some businesses they still have a place in the mix, but for most businesses these "above the line" strategies are still very expensive mediums with limited targeting ability.

The advent of social media changed this one-way communication. It gave voice to individuals, and allowed their thoughts, opinions, feelings, emotions and insights to be shared with a large audience. Instead of businesses screaming at an audience for attention, it allowed for conversation. It also enabled individuals to connect with people they had lost contact with. (In my case it provided me with a channel to interact with relatives overseas that I had never even met before.)

For most businesses these "above the line" strategies are still very expensive mediums with limited targeting ability.

FREE MARKET RESEARCH

I believe one of the greatest benefits to businesses now is that social media can actually foster *free* market research as well as customer service, the beauty of this being that if a customer is unhappy with their experience, a service, or product, they may (or likely will) use social media to voice those concerns, providing you as a business with the insight to improve the situation and/or rectify it. You need to take the good with the not so good.

As a business owner there is a huge amount of value in this. Sure, it might include a hit to the ego, or you may be concerned that bad reviews or comments will have a negative impact on your business, however what you will find is that by embracing this aspect of social media, listening and then working with your customers towards a solution, many other people will take these negative comments with a grain of salt (especially if they are a minority), and it is likely those making the complaints will even amend their comments or update them once their issues have been resolved. To be clear: there are always going to be the customers who are never happy, the ones that run off and simply attack, wanting no remedy or action, simply wanting to disparage the business. And there's not a lot you can do about that other than using social media to formulate a response that demonstrates your willingness to hear their complaint and resolve it. But, embracing this aspect of social media can bring great benefits to your business.

If this all sounds a bit much, and you think it's easier to just stay off these platforms to avoid this problem altogether, I'm sorry to say you are mistaken. Whether we like it or not, these conversations are taking place anyway, and these unhappy customers will use their own personal social media, blogs and other outlets to voice their dissatisfaction, whether your business is involved online or not. People can start their own discussions and reviews about your business on social media, and they can use multiple websites to comment about your business even if you haven't registered a listing.

As you can see, burying your head in the sand does not stop any of this from happening, and actually impacts your ability to rectify the situation and genuinely engage in productive dialogue.

YOUR CUSTOMERS NOW HAVE MORE POWER

Unfortunately, there are many businesses (both large and small) who don't do the right thing by their customers. Something that used to really upset me growing up was seeing my parents taken advantage of and feeling helpless when they had issues with businesses. I love how times have changed, and the consumer now has a powerful weapon against poor business interactions.

A number of years ago I ordered new flooring from a major national retailer for my house, which I was renovating. Unfortunately the installation of the product was woeful, causing the floorboards to crack at the corners, leaving significant visible damage. So, we gave them a courtesy call to let them know of the issues and to ask them for a solution. They agreed to come out and inspect the damage, and we were happy with that.

My wife was available to show them the issues. The franchisee and the installer came out to take a look, and in a nutshell suggested there was nothing they could really do, argued it was "barely noticeable", and even suggested we might go to the hardware store and buy some putty to try to patch up the cracks.

I bet you could imagine my reaction when I came home from work late that night to be told this. I was ropeable. How dare they make such suggestions and attempt to avoid all responsibility?

What do you think I did next?

I took to social media, posting about the situation on Facebook.

Now, at the time the store and the franchise we were dealing with didn't have a Facebook page for me to comment on. Given that I was new to the area, I aired my frustration with the store and asked if anyone I was connected to had similar issues or experiences with them. The responses started to flow, and I began to get an insight into what I could do to resolve this.

Interestingly though, a few hours later, something happened.

I received a private message on Facebook from the Head of Social Media for this retailer, with a genuine apology, his contact details, and a request for me to provide a detailed explanation for him that he would action immediately. He stated how he was sorry to hear we had a negative experience, and that as a leading retailer they take these comments very seriously.

Now, being a marketer, I can't explain how delighted I was with this. I was always aware that conversations and brand references could be monitored online, and I was pleasantly surprised that this company was actively playing a role in doing just that. (Keep in mind that social media was only about four years old at the time.)

As such, I wrote a detailed email back, firstly applauding them and their team for adopting the technology to be monitoring these conversations, and secondly to be acting on them.

The next morning I received a call from the National General Manager of Flooring for this retailer, apologising for my experience and outlining the actions they were going to take and how this issue was to be rectified. The next call I received was from the importer of the flooring product, again apologising, and advising that they would do whatever was necessary to rectify the situation, even if it meant relaying all of the floor.

Interestingly though, the next call wasn't so pleasant. It was the franchisee, who aired his disgust as to how "I could associate with such social media platforms" (as if it were some dodgy underground site), expressing anger at how I had handled this, and even having the nerve to suggest that the flooring was (technically) sold to me and not to my wife, and as such if it were that important I would have made myself available to go through the issues instead of my wife (I kid you not).

Let's just say my response shut this conversation down really quickly.

The resolution: all the floorboards were replaced where damaged. Simple.

Imagine how wrong this could have potentially gone pre–social media days. Or, even if it were rectified, how many hoops I may have had to jump through to remedy the situation. Would I have had to try to keep escalating my problem until the right person listened? Probably. And what if no-one did? What would I have done? Taken it to the ACCC? Imagine the lost time, money and energy.

You have to take the good with the bad online, and understand that you can live and die by the proverbial sword. In business we must be brave enough to own our mistakes, and be willing to do what we can to rectify them. Consumers now have a louder voice than ever, something that isn't going to change any time soon.

Ultimately social media provides businesses with the same opportunity as individuals, providing them with a "free" platform to promote their business and an insight into what they do.

Sure, many of the platforms now require advertising investment for businesses to be able to reach a larger audience, and fair enough. Ultimately they have provided a powerful marketing tool whereby all of the features are free to use – the only investment required is to reach a larger audience (through paid advertising, or "boosting", to a larger audience).

JUST ABOUT *EVERYBODY* IS ON SOCIAL MEDIA

There is one major misunderstanding I have heard time and time again when it comes to social media: "social media is just for consumers". In fact, I recall a difficult meeting with a client (who had specifically brought us in to discuss digital and social media) after they continued to repeat this line to us, despite the data and the facts we presented to them. Ultimately their opinion was respected for being just that, their opinion, but that's where it ended.

I shall elaborate and let the numbers do the talking. Social media is not just for consumers, and common sense will prevail here.

Facebook is made up of individuals. People like you and me. From celebrities through to your next-door neighbour, studies show that there will be over 2.6 billion social media users by 2018, and with an estimated global population of 7.5 billion people, that's almost 35% of the world's population using social media.

Yes, these individuals are consumers. We are *all* consumers in some form. Even at the most basic level, we all must eat, sleep and put a roof over our heads. However, we are all individuals too. We are lawyers, doctors, mechanics, accountants, police officers, marketers, entrepreneurs, engineers – the list is almost endless. What this means is that when a business thinks their audience isn't on social media, or that social media is only for consumers and consumer-type businesses, it's fair to say this is simply untrue.

So, once you accept that your target market is almost certainly on social media, no matter who they are, what comes next? What is important is understanding how your audience behaves, and establishing if social media is an appropriate platform to drive and foster engagement or develop a community, and if so, through which platform?

A great example of this is a client I consulted with who specialises in the management of assets for major clients such as universities, hospitals and government organisations. I think it's fair to say that while many of the decision makers in these organisations may well be on Facebook, for example, it is unlikely that they would use this channel or be interested in using this channel as a way of engaging with or being part of a community around asset management. What was more appropriate, however, was creating a presence on LinkedIn, using a purely business-based platform to enable dialogue surrounding this very specific topic. This way, it would be possible to establish key people within organisations who are responsible for asset management, and invite or encourage them to participate in this professional community. This is a great example of how in a business to business (B2B) environment an appropriate channel was selected (LinkedIn), and the use of the social media platform was aligned with a very specific audience. LinkedIn is by far the most popular platform when it comes to establishing business relationships and contacts. The power it provides in being able to network with and connect with professionals from all types of organisations at all levels is incredible.

MORE THAN JUST A TWO-WAY DIALOGUE

We're now going to focus on the use of engagement and community as an objective for your strategy.

Social media has enabled so much more than just a two-way dialogue. As with digital platforms such as forums, social media allows businesses to create pages which can foster a strong following, and ultimately result in a loyal community. A community is built on authenticity and forging meaningful relationships with individuals and groups alike: in essence, the formation of "tribes" who relate to and resonate with your business and want to listen to your stories.

This loyalty is the holy grail in my eyes.

Engagement is more than just "likes"

I'm often asked about the importance of the volume of "likes" (on Facebook), or followers (on Instagram, Twitter, and so on). There is an argument about volume being critical to obtain the best possible organic reach, and given that we have already established investing money into social media platforms to grow and communicate with an audience is now a mandatory component of a sound social media strategy, I still maintain this simple philosophy: would you prefer to speak to an audience of 50,000 people where only 500 of them are genuinely interested in what you have to say? Or would you rather speak to an audience of 1000 people where all of them are genuinely interested in what you have to say? The latter is my pick.

Why would you as a business want thousands and thousands of irrelevant "likes" or followers? I know I wouldn't. Common sense prevails: establishing an audience to whom your information and content is irrelevant will surely end in an exodus of your audience, who undoubtedly will want a better experience when using their social media channels. They want content to be relevant to them and tailored to their genuine interests.

When it comes to "likes" though, many businesses do think that volume is key. You can buy likes by paying someone offshore a very small fee, and then magically you would have hundreds or even thousands of followers almost overnight. If only it were that easy to build a genuine social media community. Sadly, most of these accounts would be fake accounts, used precisely for this process and offering no real benefit to your business. You'll be having a conversation with thousands of people who aren't at all interested in what you do, or who perhaps aren't even real people.

Facebook in particular is continually improving their algorithm to eliminate these accounts. Many Facebook pages that had purchased thousands of fake "likes" saw their page following drop overnight once Facebook rolled these changes out. This is an excellent move, and one that ultimately benefits all social media users.

The benefits of investing in a strong following

Now that we have established there is little value in establishing an artificial following, let's take a look at the many benefits of investing in a strong one.

Dialogue

A strong following provides you with the ability to:

- regularly converse in a two-way manner with your audience
- establish what they like and don't like

- ask for feedback on various aspects of your product or service
- build a community or a tribe whereby your followers converse among each other about your business.

Loyalty

A strong following provides you with the ability to:

- establish a community of people who are dedicated to your business, product or service
- create advocates who defend and support you within the community
- create a sense of familiarity, using insights from your business, operations and so on, to help your audience relate to you.

E-word of mouth

A strong following provides you with the ability to:

- share your message among the community, their friends, associates, and so on
- develop a following of people who want to communicate the experience and benefits of their interaction with your business
- actively seek to be spoken about through multiple digital channels.

Rating/review

A strong following provides you with the ability to:

- subject to your business type, consider requesting reviews and ratings
- make selection easier for potential customers by instilling that little bit of extra confidence when they do their research.

Promotion

A strong following provides you with the ability to:

- reward those who support you and give them a reason to keep coming back time and time again

- encourage them to share what they know about you with their peers too, and to incentivise that

- leverage your following to find other similar people who may also be interested in your business.

REAL-WORLD COMMUNITIES STILL MATTER

One thing we keep touching on, and that should be kept in mind at all times, is ultimately you must know and understand your audience. While there are opportunities for almost all businesses online, some business will be better served developing a physical community in their local marketplace, through local events, gatherings, interactions and the like. This may or may not necessitate extensive social media, subject to how your audience behaves. Try not to make assumptions about how your audience behaves, simply ask them. Ask them if they use social media, or any form of digital media, and if so, which platforms. Obtain that information firsthand. Why? Because we recently saw the 45-plus market on Facebook skyrocket. They were the fastest growing audience segment using the platform – and I couldn't tell you how many times I've heard "Facebook is for the kids". Don't make assumptions or guess at where your target market is and what they want. Find out. All the resources you need are at your fingertips.

A CHECKPOINT

In the notes section, identify three to five ways in which you could use digital or social media channels to encourage dialogue with your target audience.

NOTES:

10

UNDERSTANDING TRAFFIC

The considerations for digital traffic in the context of objective setting are threefold:

- *First:* understanding where the traffic is being generated to and from your website
- *Second:* understanding the quality of the traffic and its relevance and importance to your business
- *Third:* understanding what action you want this traffic to take.

Just like road traffic, digital or web traffic needs to be monitored and managed. How many people are coming to your website? Your Facebook page? YouTube account? Landing page? And the other online aspects of your business? Regardless of where this traffic is going to or coming from, the principles for understanding traffic are the same.

MONITORING AND UNDERSTANDING YOUR TRAFFIC

One thing you should be clear on from the beginning is that, again, setting the objective for "traffic" in isolation as an objective is not always ideal. Similar to brand awareness, traffic should be coupled with a goal, and then the data used to ascertain what is required to scale up the success of that objective, or what changes are required if the objective is not being met. For big businesses, traffic is critical, and they are reliant upon steady and growing traffic to build large audiences, which they can market to over and over again.

To explain this, let me set the scene (I am going to use website traffic as an example):

You might find that for every 1000 unique visitors to your website you receive one enquiry. What this suggests is that for every 1000 new people who come to your website, only one person enquires about your business.

Keep in mind this is hypothetical, and every industry, market and audience will have different behaviours, however this conversion would seem quite low and would suggest that there are a lot of people coming to your website but your offer, call to action, user experience or information are not compelling enough for them to take action. This allows you to identify the problem: you are getting people to your site but they are not converting, so the weakness is not attracting people to your site but having them take action once they are on the site.

Now without getting into the nitty gritty of Google Analytics (and let's assume that you already have this installed on your website – this is a must have if you're serious about digital marketing, and if you haven't done this yet I suggest you look into it immediately), if your website has a lot of information on it and your audience spends a lot of time on your website (you might find that those 1000 visitors spend an average of 10 minutes on your site), and you have no call to action – that is, the purpose of the site is to be purely informative – then perhaps receiving only one enquiry is okay?

However, for most businesses – regardless of their product or service – it is safe to say they would like to obtain some form of quantifiable action out of their website, and one enquiry out of 1000 people would definitely not be acceptable.

It all depends on what your goals are for your website, and for the particular campaign you are running. Typical goals for a website are:

- enquiries (contact, request a quote, request a call back)

- downloads (retrieve some information in exchange for details, download a product guide or an information piece, and so on)

- engagement (drive people to social media, build a following)

- sales (e-commerce sites)

- time on site reading blogs, news or articles, or watching videos

- social sharing – sending the web content out to social media sites

- database generation for the business (which would come from enquiries, downloads and sales).

All of these goals would be unachievable without traffic. If the right people aren't frequenting your site then it is unlikely you will reach any of the above outcomes. As such, the traffic objective needs a clear goal.

Where is your traffic coming from?

The first challenge in setting traffic as an objective is to understand where your digital traffic is coming from and going to. This is typically called "referral traffic". Referral traffic is traffic that has come from another digital source that can be tracked. For example, a Google AdWords campaign would create referral traffic, or a post on Facebook which has a link that takes people to your website would also be referral traffic. In other words, what sources are referring traffic to your website, landing page, Facebook page, and so on? For example, is Facebook driving the most traffic to your website? Or is your website driving the most traffic to Facebook? Is a directory listing on the internet driving lots of traffic to your website (such as Yellow Pages or True Local)? Then you also have search traffic – do most of your visitors come from searching through Google, Bing or Yahoo?

Understanding where your visitors are coming from will provide you with a better understanding of how to best amplify this. It is also a key to establishing what other digital or social strategies are worth investing in. For example, if most of your traffic is coming through search engines such as Google, there is a good chance that people are searching for a product, service, solution or answer to a question that leads them to your site. As such, it might be prudent to invest in structured search engine optimisation (SEO) to increase your prominence on these search engines to amplify the amount of traffic coming to your site. Alternatively, you might find that your audience tends to frequent Facebook regularly; as such, it could be ideal to invest in Facebook campaigns to drive traffic to your website.

If you don't know how people are coming to your site, and where they are coming from, how do you make these decisions?

Are you getting the right traffic?

The second consideration in setting traffic as an objective is to understand the quality of the visitors you are attracting and their relevance and importance to your business. Similar to what we examined when referring to your "likes" and the volume of "likes" or followers on social media, your aim is to ensure you have *the right kind of people* coming to and from your website or social pages.

Large volumes of people on your website who don't eventually become customers are not much good to your business.

Again, a great way of measuring this is through a tool such as Google Analytics (for websites) or Insights for Facebook. Within Google Analytics and Facebook Insights you are able to build a fair profile of your visitors, being able to develop an understanding of things such as their location, average age and gender. This is extremely useful in ascertaining if your marketing efforts are in line with your target.

What do you want them to do once you have them?

The third consideration in setting traffic as an objective is understanding what action you want people to take once they are on your site or social media page. Often the importance of this is overlooked. I understand there is a difference between the complexity of websites and the limitations of a social media page, however the aim here is to be thinking about the underlying principles of action once you have their attention (regardless of the medium). Ideally, what would you like your audience to do once they get to the site or social media page?

Here are some questions that require your consideration:

- Is it vital that they read every bit of information on your site before they engage with you?

- Is obtaining their contact details important?

- Do you want them to request a phone call?

- Would you like them to instantly purchase something?

- Do you want them to download resources you have created?

- Do you want them to engage in dialogue?

- Do you want them to share your content?

- Do you want them to call you immediately?

- Do you want them to send a basic enquiry?
- Do you want them to request a quote and provide the details for that quote?
- Do you want them to enter a competition?
- Do you want them to look at your images, videos, portfolio or something similar?

The answers to these questions will govern the purpose of your channels, the way in which you intend (or need) to leverage them, as well as where the traffic should come from to get the best response.

A CHECKPOINT
Using the notes section, answer the questions above. Once you have traffic coming to your website, what do you want to do with them?

NOTES:

NOTES:

PART III

BUDGETING (SHOW ME THE MONEY!)

11

TALKING ABOUT MONEY

For most financial aspects of life – be it starting or running a business, wages, investment, making large purchases – most, if not all, financial experts would encourage you to set a budget for the activity you wish to undertake. It makes sense, right?

Your marketing is no different. Whether you choose to execute these strategies internally or outsource to an agency, you don't want to be caught spending more than you intended – or more than you have – to execute your digital or social media strategies. And you will want to invest money based on a sound strategy aimed at meeting clearly defined objectives, as outlined in chapter 2.

INVESTING IN YOUR BUSINESS

There is an old adage, "You need to spend money to make money". We all know first-hand this is true, however I would challenge the word "spend". For me, this word should be changed to "invest".

I don't believe any business should "spend" money on their marketing strategies.

You might argue this is just semantics, but I disagree. Language is important, and it affects the decisions you make. A sound digital marketing and social media strategy is an investment into the well-being of your business. Just like inventory, or accounting services, or a shop front, investment into strategies that yield returns is vital to a business's ongoing success.

Keep this in mind as you read this chapter. Poorly planned and ill-informed marketing is a cost to your business. Well-thought-out and data-driven marketing is an investment in the sustainability and growth of your business.

ESTABLISHING CERTAINTY, ACCOUNTABILITY AND VALUE

In speaking with many businesses across many industries over many years, from start-ups to well-established corporations, there is always one topic that comes up: money. The difference across different sized businesses is of course the scale. Interestingly, however, I've witnessed first-hand how frugal billion-dollar businesses can be, and conversely I've seen small businesses that reinvest every bit of profit back into their marketing efforts.

In interviewing a range of businesses for this book, a common problem that many established business owners faced was money. Sound familiar? At face value, this concern surrounding money would seem as though the businesses were concerned they didn't have enough of it to invest in their marketing, but this usually wasn't the case. A little bit of investigation revealed that, for established businesses, the problem was not so much a matter of not having the money to invest but the fear of investing that money into a strategy that didn't work.

So, how can you and your business overcome this? How can you make marketing investment decisions with confidence? What tends to occur in business is that due to a lack of understanding and education surrounding digital marketing or social media investment, business owners and marketing managers struggle with three issues: certainty, accountability and value. Not understanding these issues often leads to poor marketing decisions. So, let's have a look at each of these individually, so that you can make well-informed decisions for your business.

Certainty

Many business owners are uncertain about the investment they are going to make (what they should do, how they should go about it, who to trust, and what the expectations are or should be). And, like any investment, the ability to predict outcomes or returns can be somewhat difficult. The measures outlined throughout this book – such as conducting research, being intimate with your audience and studying your traffic – will really aid in reducing the risk and uncertainty attached to the investment. Uncertainty is typically a result of a lack of knowledge or genuine understanding of what the best strategies are to implement, and whether that investment should be made in-house or outsourced.

Accountability

Being accountable for the investment being made is also key. How do you measure success? How do you calculate ROI? How do you minimise risk? Who is doing what? The money being invested into marketing or social media strategies needs to be accounted for, from the setting of budgets and objectives in relation to the investment through to the return on the investment once a strategy is implemented. It is also imperative that the professionals being engaged are accountable for the outcomes. Regardless of whether you have taken this on in-house or engaged a third-party agency, account-ability is mandatory for all involved.

Value

Achieving good value should be the underlying premise for all activity. This is something I really focus on, and I think this has helped many businesses. Speaking purely from a third-party agency perspective, I have seen it all. I have seen agencies charge management fees for campaigns that exceeded the clients' total ad budget, or engage in strategies for clients that were misaligned with their objectives just to pad their own profit (for example, the agency pushes an agenda or medium they favour, but the data suggests this is not the best medium for the client). This doesn't create any form of value for the client.

Value comes in knowing that an agency will stand by their commitments and deliverables, report religiously, and demonstrate the results of their actions. And value will hopefully come from this book, arming you with enough knowledge to ask the right questions when engaging a third party.

If you choose as a business to invest in the resource internally, the value will come from the individuals you employ and their understanding and capabilities across the breadth of digital marketing and social media activity. It is difficult for one person to "do it all" (depending on the scale of the business), in an environment where technology changes rapidly. And being across all platforms, methods and strategies is also difficult. What is important though is that one person has the ability to become intimate with the business and your audience, and so ultimately knows the right questions to ask to establish the best tactics to employ.

HANDY THINGS TO KNOW

Here's a few handy things to know, whether you choose to do this yourself or you engage an agency to execute a campaign for you:

- **Budget:** Have a clear budget in mind. A rule of thumb is to make an investment of between 2% and 10% of revenue into your total marketing activity. This percentage should then be broken up between two to four strategies that will yield the best results; for example, an SEO strategy and a social media content strategy, or a lead generation campaign with Google AdWords and a social media content strategy. The aim is to not put all of your eggs in one basket. Too many businesses rely on a single line of attack. On occasion this can work well, however many established businesses also have established, mature competitors, and they may also have varied customer segments, which means potentially different behaviours that need to be accounted for in the strategies.

- **Education:** Reading this book is already a great start. (Well done!) Arm yourself with at least the basics to be able to conduct the right discussions, be it looking to employ an internal marketing resource or engaging an external agency. Learn to establish certainty, accountability and value in your planning.

A CHECKPOINT

Using the notes section, consider nominating a budget you believe your business can afford to invest in marketing; break it down from an annual figure, to a monthly and weekly number.

NOTES:

12

HOW MUCH
SHOULD I INVEST?

I am often asked for recommendations about how much money should be invested in a particular digital marketing and/or social media strategy. This, of course, is a complicated question.

Before answering, I must first establish what a business can afford. I need some parameters to guide the answer.

My role will then be to establish the most cost-effective strategic recommendations about how to proceed to generate the best results for this individual business – to develop a campaign that works. It's really that simple. Whether it be a good internal marketing resource or an external marketing agency making the recommendations, the answer should always be the same.

When it comes to setting the budget, the rule of thumb I suggested in the previous chapter was to allocate between 2% and 10% of revenue, split between two to four activities. Of course this will vary based on things such as your products, services and channels to market. And remember, *you are only allocating what your business can afford.*

So, as you can see, there really is no straightforward answer as to how much you should invest, and I certainly can't give you a definitive answer in a book. But, what we can do is look at all of the different contributing factors, to help you work out the answer to this question for your business.

WHERE SHOULD I INVEST MY MONEY?

Do you *really* need an agency?

Often the beginning of a discussion with a potential client is when I am asked how they should best invest their money. You may be surprised to learn that on some occasions my answer is that it is not with me or my business. Sometimes there are a number of different avenues that I can ascertain (as a strategic marketer) that will yield much better results but are not a core service offering of my business; for example, perhaps a company would benefit much more from structured public relations, or perhaps by engaging an agent or distributor with a sole focus on various sales strategies, thus limiting the need for what they came to see me about.

FINDING THE BEST STRATEGY FOR YOU

A good internal marketing person or third-party agency has an obligation to develop the most effective strategies relevant to your business for the budget and resources you have available. A great way to gauge this effectiveness is to ask them how they would roll out their process and what they would recommend in the allocation of a budget.

I believe this always needs to be a "conservative first" approach. That is, you go through a process (as outlined in part IV) with an aim to create something and test it. For example, you will want to establish how the key metrics are working, establish what people respond to the most, and establish which method drives the best results. In the marketing and digital world we call this "A/B split testing". The theory can apply to almost any form of strategy or campaign.

Let's take a basic digital-only campaign, for example. Digital is fantastic for low-cost split testing. The point of split testing is to do exactly that: to create one advert that is the "control" ad, and then vary it using a different set of images, sales hooks, straplines or text, and roll that out to the same audience across the digital platforms nominated in your strategy, and then gauge which iteration the audience responds to the best. From there you would typically amplify that one advertisement, and stop the versions that didn't work so well.

The beauty about a strategy like this is threefold:

- It allows you to only invest a conservative amount of money until you understand what works best.

- It sets the baseline of the expected costs that will be attached to yielding the results you want.

- It allows you to optimise and tweak your campaign or message without a huge expense (as compared to, say, a billboard, or a TV ad, or a print ad: if you get these wrong, you've typically spent – and wasted – a lot of money!).

If you are using internal resources, work with them to justify their proposed expenditure and link the results back to your expected returns (be it data, leads, sales, and so on). If you are using a third-party agency, work with them to help them understand the value you are seeking. Be transparent with them in demonstrating key metrics such as your average sale value, or the importance of a lead to a business. You can even make comparisons against other methods you may have implemented before. Be open about the success or failure of what you've done previously; evaluate exactly what you did, how much you invested, and why you believed it worked or did not.

I hope that a common theme is resonating here as you read through the chapters of this book. Regardless of the size of your business, the size of your marketing budget and the resources you have at hand, your approach should be strategic, methodical and focused. Invest what you can wisely, and in a manner that allows you to measure and be accountable for the results.

A CHECKPOINT

Using the notes section, and considering the information provided about SMART objectives and objective setting, confirm what your budget is, and think about the two to four activities you could consider implementing.

NOTES:

NOTES:

13

CALCULATING RETURN ON INVESTMENT

I presume by now we have established that everything you do must be accounted for. I understand it sounds like common sense but it's often overlooked. Careful measurement and accounting plays a vital role when making strategic decisions about the money your business needs to invest in its digital and social activity. In this chapter we will touch on different ways to calculate the return on your investment (ROI) for this activity, both the tangible and intangible.

OBJECTIVES AND ROI

Part II of this book (looking at objectives) is critical to understanding ROI, which can be measured against a number of different outcomes. If you don't have clear objectives in place for your digital marketing and social media activity, you will have no way to accurately assess whether you are achieving a positive return on your investment.

A great example of this is a client I work with who has a leading product in the market. They have numerous competitors, and they also have an "identity crisis", whereby people use their brand name to describe the product they are looking for. As such, all variations of the product in the market are branded or positioned around this name, yet their product is the true product, the original product. It's like people saying "Kleenex" when referring to a tissue, or "Thermos" when referring to a flask, or "Esky" when referring to a cooler. The marketing challenge here, though, is not so much the mix up of terminology but helping consumers understand that their brand name or product name is superior, and to distinguish between this product and the remaining products in the market which is saturated with other competitor products, making it difficult for a consumer to discern the differences between the options available.

Their marketing objective however is to gain leads. These leads are typically generated via digital platforms, whereby a potential customer is educated about the differences between their product and the competitor products on the market. These leads are then fed to preferred "resellers", whose job is to service the customer direct in their locality.

A such, there are two main objectives for this client:

- The first objective is to build a level of interest and brand awareness for the brand so that the product name being coined and their product are immediately associated together. In other words, when someone looks to identify this product, they are positioned as the original, best and most appropriate product in the market. (Just like if someone looks for Kleenex, or an Esky, they will find the Kleenex Brand and the Esky Brand products.)

- The second objective is cold, hard leads of qualified people who are actively interested in obtaining a price for the product in their area. These leads could be by way of website enquiries or phone calls.

As there are two distinct objectives, ROI can be measured in different ways, and the correct return needs to be attributed to each objective.

The first objective we touched on is brand awareness (see part II), and how this can be created by providing valuable content to the target market. With this client we ticked this box by creating a series of videos, landing pages and useful copy and images that clearly demonstrate why our client's product is the superior product.

The ROI here revolves around the resources being attributed to create quality content that is valuable to the consumer, and ultimately enables the brand to be positioned favourably on Google (in other words, the branding and the business ranks high in Google when the product term is being searched for).

ROI is calculated by measuring the amount invested in the creation of this content, divided by the amount of organic traffic coming to the site ("organic traffic" is that which occurs naturally without using a paid campaign). Some marketers may argue this is more so a "cost per click" metric and not a return, however I would argue that initial return is in fact that the attention has been given to you (and the traffic, which is important to your site) because the content is valuable, is ranked high on Google, and as such drives an audience to review the content, your website and your product. For example, it might require an investment of $1000 to create the content that drives the organic traffic; if that piece of content drives 100 users to your website, the return here is one user's attention for every $10 invested.

This first objective is then used to drive the second objective: leads. These are created by generating the right traffic, aimed at capturing our target audience who has a particular problem or need, and establishing our client is the solution to that problem or need through the content and conversation we have created through our brand awareness objective. The people who learned about the product through the content were driven to the website, and then they needed to part with their details to obtain a quote on a market-leading product.

To calculate the ROI here, we would take the total dollar value invested in the content (in this example let's stick with $1000) and divide it by the number of enquiries we received: let's say out of the 100 users who came to the site, 10 of them enquired and so provided their details. This means that the return here is one person's details for every $100 invested.

Now I get it; by this stage you still haven't made a physical sale, and you could say, "Well, what good is that? I've just invested $1000 to get 100 users and 10 potential customer details." It is vital that you are aware of the value you have at this point in time (that is, before the sale is even made). In this instance:

- We have attracted and gained 100 people's attention.

- We have 100 unique users, and digital marketing gives us the ability to capture and remarket to them (see chapter 8).

- This audience enables you to build profiles of other audiences that are similar and that can be used for future prospecting.

- We have 10 potential customer details which enables you to create regular conversations with them, provide them with an offer and incentive, and provide outstanding and superior customer service to them, taking them on a journey to tell your story and to a sale.

The point that is most valuable here is the way in which we need to look at attention and why it's becoming ever so important when you actually manage to capture someone's attention, and then enable them to act. I hope this helps set the scene on the way in which ROI can be viewed and should be evaluated when engaging in marketing, digital and social strategies. (Refer back to the importance of "paid, owned, earned" in chapter 6.)

CRUNCHING THE NUMBERS

Keeping things simple, four of the most common ways to calculate ROI are:

- the cost per acquisition
- the cost of a lead
- the cost of a conversion
- the profit made on a sale.

Let's have a look at each of these.

The cost per acquisition

This is by far the first and most important "bottom line" metric. Cost per acquisition is focused on the cost of turning someone into a customer; ultimately, what it cost you as a business to make them purchase from you. These costs should be assessed per campaign ideally, which enables you to value a specific activity and the result it derived. This in turn will allow you to compare it against other activities, allowing you to choose where your investment should be shifted.

There are a few calculations in this metric to calculate the cost per acquisition and ultimately its true value to the business.

The first part is working out the actual cost per acquisition:

$$\text{Cost per acquisition} = \frac{\text{Total cost of campaign}}{\text{Number of people who purchased}}$$

For example, if you spent $10,000 on a campaign, and you made 100 sales, that's a cost per acquisition of $100.

The second part of this equation revolves around what this number (100 sales) actually means to your business. If, for example, those sales were $10 each, then the return is clearly unacceptable (you only made $1000 in sales), however if the sales were $100 each then you broke even, and if the sales were $1000 each, you've made $90,000 (less the total campaign cost).

Of course, these numbers need to be assessed, perhaps with your accountant, marketing manager or CFO, to accurately establish the profitability and true value of the campaign. For example, many businesses tend to remove the "management" component of the campaigns from these calculations (and only attribute the ad spend), simply because they understand that they would need to employ the resources (which would become an overhead) in order to execute these campaigns, and as such they would prefer to engage the external experts who are tasked with simply getting results.

The cost of a lead

The easiest way to calculate ROI on a marketing campaign is to take the dollar amount of the investment and divide it by the number of leads obtained during the period being examined (be it for a month, year or another time period):

$$\text{Cost per lead} = \frac{\text{Total campaign investment (\$)}}{\text{Number of leads}}$$

Let's consider another example: a client I worked with who sold very specific courses for a high-end target market. The course cost was $25,000 per person to attend, and the average profit from each attendee was $10,000.

Let's work out the value of each lead for this business.

Even the most ambitious and aggressive of marketing people would suggest that if you can achieve a 10:1 ROI then you are in a great place. A 10:1 ROI suggests that for every dollar you invest, you receive 10 dollars in return. As such, in this example, each lead could cost up to $1,000 to attain and you would have an excellent result. In our case, we achieved a cost of $150 per lead, which is a 66:1 result – nothing short of exceptional. On average, an ROI of 2:1 or greater is a more than acceptable result. Subject to your average margin, a 2:1 ROI means you are doubling your money invested at the very least.

This calculation is a great way to establish the cost of each lead to your business and therefore ascertain if the lead is worth the investment. Often, businesses tend to think that the cheaper the lead the better, and while of course it is ideal to keep the cost per lead as low as possible, this should not be the only consideration. You also need to consider acquisition, which is the act of that person actually making a purchase, and the profit derived from that purchase (see cost per acquisition above).

The cost of a conversion

The next measure of return would be the value of the "conversion", which ascertains the cost per action that you determine. In other words, it tells you how much money you needed to spend in order to get that action. An action could be someone filling out an enquiry form (meaning the value is in their details), an action could be a phone call, it could be the download of a piece of content, and so on. A conversion is effectively any goal you set that you want a user to do.

$$\text{Cost per conversion} = \frac{\text{Total campaign investment (\$)}}{\text{Number of conversions}}$$

Of course, if the cost of conversion exceeds the value of the actions generated in total – and provided there were no other metrics that were important or valuable to you, such as lead generation or an entry-level (small value) purchase to capture them into your funnel – the strategies being used would require re-evaluation.

Calculating profit on a sale

You can then take this one step further. Subject to your business's ability to then track and monitor sales that have been generated, you can then also calculate ROI from the campaign to ascertain the profit generated from your marketing activities. The calculation would be:

$$\frac{\text{Gross profit from sales generated (\$) – Total marketing investment (\$)}}{\text{Marketing investment}} = \text{Profit per sale}$$

Once you know these figures, you will have a perfect understanding of the amount of money you should invest in order to generate an acceptable return according to your objectives for a campaign.

GETTING THE WHOLE PICTURE

The goal for calculating return on investment is to understand the holistic picture of what you are getting in return for the money being spent. The other side of this equation is evaluating the investment being made in either outsourcing the support through a third-party agency or employing a full-time marketing resource who then manages the work either entirely or with a combination of external resources.

This is a critical factor that needs to be considered as a business owner or manager. Your time is extremely valuable, and as such the savings to the business, the requirement to minimise overheads and the benefit of employing experts are all factors that are relevant in evaluating your ROI.

A CHECKPOINT

Using the notes section, if you have run campaigns before, why not attempt calculating the various metrics as outlined? Or, if you haven't undertaken campaigns, consider how you would use these when setting a budget for a campaign and knowing the outcome you would require in order to justify the investment.

NOTES:

PART IV

THE SIX STEPS FOR SUCCESS (HERD SHEEP NOT CATS)

It sounds like a cliché, but every good business has a framework – a strategy or process that it follows rigorously, a system that ensures your investment is being treated with the respect and attention it deserves. As a marketer, everything I do follows these steps. This is by no means revolutionary, just a simple six-step process that ensures that strategies and tactics are developed and delivered in a methodical way that we know produces great results.

14

STEP 1: ANALYSE

Analyse. A word some may shudder at, or perhaps for many business owners this is all they do. Regardless of your feelings, analysis is where all great marketing journeys begin.

All too often I engage in meetings where there is a tendency to jump straight to tactics (we've covered this earlier in the book), without first considering the objectives or analysing the available information so as to make better decisions about the tactics to be employed. I get it; we live in an age where we are exposed to so many platforms, techniques, solutions, strategies and telemarketers selling us "guaranteed ways to be number one on Google". But, how do we know what will *really* work? How should we go about making the most strategic of decisions, to develop the best approach and ideally the best return?

It starts with an analysis. This can be as complicated or as simple as you like. The key is to use research and data to aid in the decision-making process, so that you're not just taking a guess, "having a crack" at something or implementing a plan just because it's the latest fad.

The great news for most businesses is that market research, data and other information about your audience, markets and so on is readily available. Presuming as an established business you already have the basics in place such as a website, or perhaps you are already doing some social media, SEO, pay per click or other basic marketing activities, you will also have access to a range of your own useful data to help you make strategic decisions.

Diving into the analytics and the numbers can help add a lot of insight into your industry and what you are doing that is already working. After all, you are an established business, you are already making money, and you are ready to take things to the next level – you just need to know how to amplify what you are currently doing.

GATHERING THE DATA

Let's take a look at some of the numbers that are available, either free or at a reasonable cost:

1   **Industry reports:** Companies such as IBISWorld provide excellent insights into a particular industry and its respective market segments. They can provide data on:

    ▪   market size

    ▪   market makeup

    ▪   the big players

    ▪   where the market is at in the business life cycle.

    This information serves as an excellent foundation to build a business case.

2   **Your website:** If you don't have Google Analytics installed, ask your web developer to do this yesterday and to provide

you with access. There are a tonne of videos online that can show you how to use the Google Analytics data. You can gain a wonderful insight into things such as:

- how many people have visited your site
- where they have come from to get to your site (search, referred, campaigns, and so on)
- how long they stayed on your site (indicating if they are reading your content or not)
- how many were new visitors versus returning visitors (very valuable if you need regular new visitors coming to the site, or conversely if you want an audience that regularly uses the website)
- the age, gender and location of your visitors (critical when understanding your target audience)
- if they reached your site from a search engine, you can find out what keywords they searched
- how many pages they viewed when on your site – did they get past the first page, or did they click around?

3   **Your social media:** If you have adopted a basic social media strategy, each of the platforms typically has some form of data attached to it that you can review. Facebook in particular has a great reporting system that shows you things such as:

- reach (how many people have seen your content)
- clicks (how many people have clicked on your content)
- engagement rate (the percentage of followers or people who have seen your content and who have interacted with it through comments, "likes", shares, and so on)
- "likes" (how many people "like" your page)

- audience (how old your followers are, what time of day they use the platform, what days of the week they are most active, and so on).

4 **Your current customers:** Starting internally is always a great idea before trying to research an external market. You can do everything from conducting a simple survey through to having one-on-one discussions with your customers to gain some insights. You could evaluate:

- Who are your current customers?

- How did they find you?

- Where do they come from?

- How often do they buy from you?

- Why do they buy from you?

- How much do they spend on average?

- How old are they?

- What gender are they?

- What are their interests?

- What do your customers have in common?

5 **Industry bodies:** Most large industries collate and release information on their members and the industry as a whole. This is valuable when selling into the industry or if you are working within the industry. Similar to data from companies such as IBISWorld but aligned with a governing body, you can gain excellent insights into:

- the key companies within an industry

- the value of an industry

- the legislation and requirements within the industry

- the networks and resources within an industry

- the people within the industry
- the job titles within the industry.

6   **Australian Bureau of Statistics:** Often overlooked as a source for data, the ABS has mountains of gold when it comes to issues such as the economy, property trends and ownership, wages, health, and the current status of the country as a whole.

7   **Online tools:** There are a host of online tools available for gathering great insights and data on your target audience and their behaviours too. For example, Google has excellent tools to help you ascertain how many searches are conducted daily for a particular keyword or phrase.

DIVING INTO THE DATA

So what do you do with the data once you have it? Well, without going into a monologue on market research, it's really quite simple: focus on your target audience and your target industry, crunch the numbers on the data that is relevant to the campaign you are planning, and bring that information together to make better strategic decisions about what is happening within your area of focus. Once you have that analysis, you are then well positioned to strategise. You'll be making well-informed decisions based on data from a number of different sources, and not just trying something on a whim or because it seems like the latest trend.

A CHECKPOINT

Use the notes section to consider what you can analyse in your business and what you can learn from that information.

NOTES:

15

STEP 2: STRATEGISE

Once you have analysed the relevant information at hand, you've effectively undertaken a form of market research that is going to guide and govern your digital marketing and social media strategies. Whether you employ someone in-house or outsource this to an agency, this is the area of most value to a business; ultimately the core of the marketing profession is someone who can distil the market research and analysis, and then establish a series of core strategies that will (based on the numbers) yield the biggest impact and returns.

Using data to make sound strategic decisions is critical in mitigating the risk attached to your marketing investment. Of course, we have already established that we can't always predict exactly how an audience will respond or the actions they will take, however we can ensure that every measure we put in place and our strategy is aligned in a way that seamlessly integrates with the way our target audience thinks, acts and behaves, thus maximising our chances of success.

Strategising comes in a number of forms. I know when I do it with my clients, I typically run workshops that go from two hours to a full day, or we do teleconferences, or if it's internal and my agency is tasked with providing the strategies, we might get together as a team or on a call and go through a range of ideas to suit each objective. And that's the key here: setting a strategy that is based on your objectives, and more importantly, following it through.

GETTING DOWN TO BUSINESS

Sound marketing strategies are typically short or long term. Let's have a look at how they differ.

Short-term strategies

Short-term strategies typically revolve around a highly concentrated "push" or "drive" in a particular area, among a very specific audience, with a focus on a particular service or product offering, and they usually last no more than one to three months.

Where I have seen short-term marketing strategies work quite well is with established businesses that are already kicking goals in particular areas but they want to amplify a specific area of their business. Their business is typically already well known, they have a great database of customers, and they know the areas of their business that drive the best returns.

The reason short-term marketing strategies tend to work so well with established businesses is that – as we've already discussed – modern marketing theory suggests that on average it takes around 12 "touches" for an individual to take action. (A "touch" can be a piece of information, an ad, a video, content, a download – basically anything that exposes your audience to your brand and message.) As such, an established business has already touched an audience in a variety of ways, and so is likely to yield quicker results with less investment as opposed to starting from scratch. Hence the effectiveness of short-term strategies for established businesses.

Some examples of short-term marketing strategies are:

- **referral lead generation campaigns:** aimed at leveraging current customers to drive an influx of new leads for database growth

- **electronic direct mail (EDM):** offering an immediate promotion, offer, gift or important information, with a strong call to action (CTA) to drive an immediate response

- **trade shows:** being present at a trade display, with the aim of securing a number of meetings in order to network

- **ad campaigns:** for example, a pay per click (PPC) strategy aimed at driving immediate traffic to a landing page or similar; alternatively, it could be a Facebook or Instagram campaign aimed at achieving a similar objective

- **media blasts:** this could be a PR stunt or a release of articles to the media, something that is relevant, time bound and serves a purpose of generating immediate interest.

Long-term strategies

As the name suggests, long-term strategies are designed with a future play in mind. They are strategies that require time to gain traction. While the definition of "long term" is somewhat varied, in my experience, and based on the rapidly changing marketing environment, long term is one to three years on average.

Subject to the industry, the customers, the market, the segments, and the objectives for your business, long-term strategies are about a goal that is designed to create a strong foundation, awareness and ongoing business, and they ensure that you are focused and consistent on where the business needs to be and what you are required to do to achieve this. Long term is not aiming for a "one-hit wonder", it's about consistency – consistency in your messaging, consistency in the stories you tell your audience, consistency in the audience you target, and consistency in the brand and the experience your audience receives when dealing with you.

Some examples of long-term marketing strategies are:

- **A rebrand of the business:** For example, you may have been established for 10 years and your brand, the market and your competitive landscape have changed, rendering you dated. Over the next year you could take your customers and your target audience on a journey while you rebrand (and potentially reposition) yourself in the marketplace.

- **Community building:** The importance of community has now become more prominent than ever. From the caveman days people have formed tribes, and today tribes still form and grow into loyal communities. This is a continual process. It doesn't happen overnight – it tends to take one to three years to grow a strong and vibrant community.

- **Content building:** The importance of content has never been more obvious. And not just any content: *valuable* content that is useful to your audience. Careful content curation, placement and dissemination is a valuable long-term strategy. It can aid in your business ranking highly on Google (organic traffic), and it also helps to build trust, relationships and credibility.

- **Database building:** While this can be done in smaller short-term chunks, it is also a long-term strategy as it requires a focus on guiding people to enter your business at the "top of the funnel"; that is, attracting them through various sources designed to take them on a journey with the aim of converting them in the future.

Many strategies can (and should) be broken down into smaller tactics and short-term goals, to make the process more manageable while still providing support for stable growth.

STICKING TO YOUR GUNS

Regardless of the short- or long-term strategies employed, one thing I implore you to do is stick with it. Often businesses are romanced by the idea of lots of sales, lots of customers and lots of business, yet many are not ready to scale properly in a way that can service their audience well and achieve these goals over the longer term.

I am not saying stand by and watch your money get thrown away in the hope that something works when clearly it's not. Sometimes even well-planned strategies don't achieve the outcome we desire. What I do want to get across is that it's important to be prepared to give the strategies the time they require to prove successful.

In my early days of agency land working with small clients, I sometimes fell into the trap of bending to their needs as opposed to sticking to what I knew worked. On occasion we would be only days into a campaign and, because it hadn't immediately generated a result, the pin was pulled or the client asked us to change tack. I quickly learnt this wasn't the right kind of business nor the right kind of client for me. However, the most valuable lesson it taught me was to set an expectation with a client: it's like the difference between preparing for a bus trip and preparing for a pilgrimage. With a bus trip there is no major preparation: you pay for your ticket and it will take you from A to B. This is unlike a pilgrimage, for which you need to be prepared: prepared to dig in, prepared for the unknown, prepared for all situations, and prepared to mitigate potential risks along the way. The same applies to marketing strategies and campaigns: being prepared is the analysis, and then being ready to follow through on the pilgrimage is the campaign.

A CHECKPOINT

Use the notes section to identify the ways in which you can use the long-term strategies identified in this chapter in your own business.

NOTES:

NOTES:

16

STEP 3: CREATE

I love this bit.

It's where science and art combine.

It's where the objectives we have set, the data we have gathered, the insights we have uncovered and the strategies are ready for execution. Of course, I could write an entire book just on creation: the channels to use, the types of campaigns, the collateral, advertisements – it goes on and on. However, in this chapter I thought it would be worthwhile to simply go through each of the main digital marketing channels and identify what is involved in the creation process for each. The reason I am not covering off on traditional marketing creation is that it's fair to say this is understood by most businesses. Businesses understand, for example, that for a print campaign you require a copywriter to write the content of the campaign, a graphic designer to design the advertisement to the specifications required, and then of course the print medium to place the advertisement (such as a magazine or newspaper). It's pretty straightforward.

The digital space, however, tends to come with more questions and a little more complexity. This chapter is aimed at simplifying this to arm you as a businesses owner with enough knowledge to make good decisions around the strategies and tactics you employ here, or that are being recommended to you. So let's have a look at the many different platforms and techniques you will come across in this growing and ever-changing world.

YOUR WEBSITE

This is typically where it all begins. Occasionally businesses may not require a website as their goals or objectives are specifically based around communities, and as such they can use social media platforms as their main presence. For the majority of us, however, the website is the foundation for everything we do online.

A website is no longer simply a digital version of your corporate brochure or a single page that tells viewers to pick up the phone. A website is now a critical business tool; in fact, it should be treated as a capital expense and an asset for your business.

An underlying premise for your website should be: "What can I do to make my customers'/clients'/users' lives easier?"

Your website has four main objectives:

- **To tell your story.** Your customers (potential or existing) need to be taken on a journey when they enter your site. They need to understand what you do really quickly. They need their questions answered, and they need to feel that you are the right business to help them solve the problem they are having.

- **To give your visitors a purpose.** What is your call to action? What should they do while they are on your site? Do you want them to get a quote? Or if they are going to send in their details, why should they? Are they going to watch some videos? Are they going to search your products? Visitors to your website require a purpose, and how you design your site plays an important role in achieving that. The site doesn't need to be overly flashy or have lots of bells and whistles. Just make it clean, clear, simple, easy to read, easy to navigate and easy to find the information they are after. Just because you have an amazing looking site doesn't mean people are going to come to you in droves. It has to be useful.

- **To give your visitors as much as you think they need.**
  If they need information to make the sales process easier, give it to them. If they need downloads of samples, guides or instructions, give these to them. If they need to make an appointment, make this easy. If they want someone to give them a call back, make this a simple process. Keep your audience in mind at all times and give them what they require to make educated and informed decisions, and to take action.

- **Conversion.** Every website should have goals attached to it. If it's people watching a video, if it's enquiries, if it's sales – it doesn't matter what the actual goal is, there needs to be a measurable objective that yields a conversion of some form.

FACEBOOK

As the market-leading social media platform, Facebook is one of the most effective advertising platforms that exists today. Its value lies in the customer insights and the user data that is collected continually.

Facebook has a primary goal of making your experience as a user as timely and as relevant as possible. It wants to ensure that the content you are exposed to is of relevance and of interest to you. As such, businesses and the ability of business pages to reach their audience organically (meaning without paid advertising) have been penalised in the process, and rightly so. I find it amusing how some business owners who were given such a powerful and free platform to build their communities got all up in arms the minute Facebook chose to reduce organic reach for business pages, and ultimately advised that if you wanted to be seen, you needed to pay to ensure the message you are paying to show is aligned with what your target audience wants. I mean, c'mon – prior to social media you had almost no choice but to pay to advertise your business. Even the simplest of listings in the *Yellow Pages* (remember that big, heavy book that got delivered to your door each year?) cost a pretty penny. Printing brochures, leaflets, cards, posters and sending out direct mail and letters cost money. So suck it up. If you want to invest in a social media strategy, be prepared to invest in building your community on it too.

Without going into the ever-changing details of all the types of ads available through the Facebook platform, the principles are simple:

- You select an objective (for example, generating "likes", video views or website traffic).
- You then select the specific audience you wish to target.
- You establish what interests your audience has that make your ad relevant to them.
- You allocate a location, a timeframe and a budget for your campaign.

And you're good to go.

For your campaign to be effective, your creative content (images, videos, slideshows, and so on) and your message (hooks, straplines, calls to action) need to appeal to your audience immediately. You have an approximately one- to three-second window (data varies on this according to different studies, but you get the picture – it's short) to capture their attention and get them to act. People have a tendency to draw conclusions between the "stimulus" (images and words) and their interests. If these two don't align perfectly, you will find you end up wasting a lot of time and money.

People are now known to "snack" on content. We scroll, and we scroll quickly. No longer are people interested in reading three-page articles; well, not during their initial exposure anyway. The carrot needs to be dangled, and an appetiser for the message needs to tell enough, really quickly, to gain their attention. That attention can then be converted into the action (or objective) you have set. And if you have done it right, expect results. You can expect to generate a lot of web traffic, which you can then remarket to (remarketing is explained in chapter 8; in essence, remarketing allows you to 'capture' visitors to your website, and then proceed to show them your advertisements as they navigate around the web or social media sites), or generate qualified leads, or have your video viewed.

LINKEDIN

As a growing platform that has evolved around professional profiles for individuals and company pages, while providing a platform for networking, content delivery and being effectively an online résumé, LinkedIn also has an advertising platform attached to it.

The advertising platform is still quite limited as to what can and can't be done, and I have experienced mixed results with its performance. Where I have found the most value is in creating a great article, piece of content or compelling link to a website, and then using the advertising platform to promote that content to a very specific audience.

If you sell educational courses, or marketing automation software, or products or services relevant to professionals who would be frequenting LinkedIn regularly then it would serve as an appropriate channel. The principles are similar to Facebook: your messages should be relevant to the audience you are targeting.

INSTAGRAM

Instagram is proving to be an extremely valuable advertising platform. It's reliant on the impact of the image, video or carousel to capture attention.

Instagram was designed as a purely visual medium (with little to no text) with the use of "hashtags". A "hashtag" is where a word, phrase, acronym or saying is used with a "#" in front of it. This allows users of the social media platform to follow a particular topic or trend associated with that hashtag. For example, #TBT stands for "throwback Thursday" and can be used when people are posting old images or videos.

Instagram is owned by Facebook and uses the Facebook advertising platform to create and advertise on it. Similar to the Facebook ads, you can set particular objectives that are designed to encourage a particular action, such as video views, app installs, website traffic or page following.

Creativity is key here, and with such an emphasis on visually appealing media you need to make sure your content really stands out.

GOOGLE

Google is the number one search engine in the world. Most of you would know that of course. What has made it so successful is that it was built to do one thing, and one thing *really* well. When you go to the home page of Google, you only have one thing to do: search. That's it.

Google (and most search engines) are effectively broken up into two sections:

- *paid*, whereby you use their advertising platform to pay for presence

- *organic*, whereby your website ranks on the search engine organically (that is, without paying).

AdWords (paid)

Once you search, you are greeted with a plethora of search items that are designed to be the most relevant sources of information based on what you are looking for, highly tailored to your location, the keywords you used, and the information on the sites that best matches what you are looking for.

At the very top of the search page, though, are paid advertisements. Otherwise known as pay per click (PPC), Google AdWords hosts a number of different paid advertising options, helping your business to be found. The Google AdWords advertising offering can be broken down as follows:

- search

- display

- pre-roll

- remarketing

- shopping.

Let's have a look at each of these.

Search

This is where your chosen keywords are used to show your ad at the top of a page search in Google. For example, if you search "local mechanic", it is likely that one of the businesses in your area (or a well-known franchise) has a Google AdWords paid search campaign that is aimed at getting you to either call the business or visit their website to make a booking or enquiry.

These ads are text-based only, and are designed to promote action (call or click). They can be used to offer a promotion or a discount, or communicate an important message.

Display

Display uses the Google AdSense platform, whereby websites that yield high traffic volumes (lots of visitors every day) allocate space on their web pages for the use of banner advertising. These ads yield these companies ad revenue, in exchange for having a popular site with targeted audiences. A great example of websites that support display ads are Gumtree, eBay and a number of the big news sites.

Similar to search ads, if you use this form of advertising your graphical banners will display on these websites that your target audience is frequenting. You can even match these display placements with keywords to make the ads more relevant to the audience.

Pre-roll

Controlled by Google, pre-roll ads are the advertising videos you see before you watch a YouTube video. They come up at the beginning, and they are typically created using a specific methodology to entice action (for example, someone clicking on the video or the link before they get to the video they were about to watch). These ads work great with visual mediums, and Google allows you to place your ads on the most relevant videos that generate a lot of views. For example, if you had a company selling accessories for boats, you could create a video ad that allows you to place that video in front of all of the "how to" videos about boating on YouTube.

Remarketing

As we've already looked at, remarketing or retargeting is a technique used on digital platforms such as Google and Facebook. The premise of remarketing is really quite simple: it uses a snippet of website code inserted into your website to "capture" visitors who come to your site. Then what happens is that either Google or Facebook (whichever you have set up your remarketing on) displays your ads to that audience while they are online. Once you are aware of the technique you will notice it often. For example, if you go to a site such as Whereis, or even eBay or Gumtree, and then you go on to Facebook or on to another website that uses Google Display campaigns, you may well start to see ads for the websites or the products you have just visited, and then continue to see them multiple times.

The difference between remarketing and retargeting is small. While the terminology is similar, remarketing is typically used on ecommerce platforms, where the website captures the product someone has just viewed and then continues to show that product across other digital platforms. Retargeting is typically used for pure advertisements: someone clicks on your ad, visits your website, and then continues to see your ads when they are on other websites.

Shopping

Many of you would have been exposed to Google shopping on numerous occasions. Specifically, when you search a specific product or a part number for a product, if the product and brand you are after is being marketed digitally and is sold online, it is likely that you will see this product arise under the Google Shopping component of Google, which falls under the AdWords offers.

Businesses, and especially ecommerce websites, use Google Shopping as a great way to gain rankings for products, which Google will then use to direct people to your site. This allows a user to go straight from the search to the right product and purchase it immediately. Google charges businesses for this product image and link placement.

Search engine optimisation (organic)

Search engine optimisation (SEO), in simple terms, is the way in which search engines (such as Google) find, rank and reference your site when people search for particular keywords and phrases. This is known as an organic ranking, which means it comes up in Google in the main search results (somewhere, but ideally on page one) and doesn't require money to be listed. In other words, you can't buy the number one organic ranking on Google. If anyone promises you this, run a million miles away. No-one can guarantee it. Google's algorithm is an ever-changing beast, measuring hundreds of thousands of factors all the time to ensure what it brings up is accurate and relevant to the search. What you *can* buy, however, is a structured, well-researched and content-based approach to SEO, with an aim to improve your rank organically for keywords and phrases. Put simply, it's not an accident that your site will rank well.

SEO has evolved greatly over the years; as the sheer volume of content on the internet expands, the complexity of people's searches has adapted to suit. People don't usually just search for single words. Typically people search for phrases, or questions, and they seek information that answers their problem.

SEO in simple terms is broken up into two components:

- **Technical:** This is quite straightforward. A good website developer will help ensure that your website meets all the criteria from Google to be SEO compliant. There are a number of technical requirements that need to be built into a site to ensure that it is set up in a way that it will be found. These include things such as site speed, your webmaster tools, site map submission and H1 tags. Don't know what these are?

That's okay. Ask your web developer about these components, and take the time to understand what they come back with.

- **Content:** This is the most critical component of SEO activity in my opinion. In essence, your website content needs to answer and deliver responses to what people are looking for. Sounds easier than it is, however the goal of SEO is to help provide valuable, creative, informative content that appeals to and is relevant to the person searching. Google places emphasis on establishing trust, and uses a number of parameters to establish if the content being found is of relevance and is of value to the person searching.

Unfortunately, SEO is another one of the offerings in the marketing sphere that has been grossly abused and delivered by some dodgy operators. I recall in my early days clients would ask me for an SEO cost proposal, and they would receive something back that was usually in the vicinity of four digits. Their response was often that they had a company in India, the US or Europe quote a small three-figure sum to "do the same thing". However, those who took the time to understand what we deliver for their investment realised that the sheer resources that go into a lot of the "grunt work" to do this properly (research, writing, graphic design, outreach) quickly add up, and that the results are commensurate with the investment made.

What the others also didn't realise was that there are two types of SEO: whitehat and blackhat techniques. The names themselves suggest which is "good" and which is "bad".

Whitehat, as the name suggests, is like an online "angel" whereby the techniques used by the SEO team are designed to be qualified, sustainable, strategic actions that result in output (such as quality content) that Google will favour and, as such, will push your website up the ranks.

Blackhat, similarly, is the online "devil" whereby the techniques created are aimed at "tricking" (or "gaming") Google into *thinking* that your website is valuable, and you are getting loads of traffic, and lots of links. But very quickly Google will pick up on this and establish that it is being tricked. As a result, Google will do one of two things: it will de-rank your website, pushing it far down the list (well beyond the first 10 results pages, on average), and secondly (worst case), it will "black list" your website, which means it stops "crawling" your site, which is what enables it to be found in searches. This is typically what you get when you employ these cheap tactics.

I have had a few clients over the years who have come to me after they have been down the wrong path, typically driven by budgetary restraints or simply because the sales call was so convincing and the results seemed too good to ignore – until their site was shut down.

When you are looking for a business to engage that offers SEO as a service, ask them about their methods. Ask them if they put a strategy together first, and what that strategy looks like. Ask them about their content production process and how they do their research. And ask them what KPIs they will set and what you as a customer can expect to receive. If you're not happy with any of their responses, this isn't the right company for you.

Content curation

Content is king. That's been touched on throughout the book, and we cover this in detail in chapter 7, however I have specifically added content into this section as good content is what will underpin all of the digital advertising strategies you employ, and is vital to a good ranking on Google.

There are many forms of content that can be created – here's just a few:

- infographics
- listicles
- blogs
- videos
- podcasts
- webinars

- audio recordings
- display ads
- pre-roll videos
- social media graphics, images and posts
- PDF whitepapers.

One thing to always keep in mind is that there is *a lot* of content out there already, so ask yourself what you are doing that is different. What questions are you answering that aren't being answered out there already? Or if there is already similar content out there, how can you create content that is more up to date, exciting and enticing to engage with?

ELECTRONIC DIRECT MAIL

Once you have built a database – or for the more advanced among us, you might have a pipeline of users at different stages in your database, each of which can be segmented differently and communicated to in different ways – electronic direct mail (EDM) is a great strategy for connecting with your audience in a direct and valuable manner.

Where many companies tend to go wrong with EDM is that they treat it like any other email and don't provide anything of interest or of value to the reader. We all get bombarded with dozens or even hundreds of emails each day (I know I do), and as such you want a compelling reason to open an email, right?

The key to success is in the strapline (the subject line of the email). The subject line is all you really have to grab the attention of your audience and to entice action, so make it worthwhile, catchy and relevant to your audience. There are lots of stats out there about average open rate percentages that show how EDM campaigns perform on average, and you can use these stats to gauge if you're on the right track or not. You can also test and measure your own campaigns, to see what works best.

SUMMARY OF THE PURPOSE OF EACH PLATFORM

Understanding the purpose of each platform, and the way an audience behaves in relation to each, will help you understand the best way in which to utilise and leverage them.

Here is a summary for each:

- **Your website:** this is typically the hub of your digital and online activity. It's the one place where a user can comfortably do their due diligence on your business, review your products or services, learn about you, your offer, your points of difference, perhaps even purchase direct from you, contact you and engage with your content.

- **Facebook and LinkedIn:** designed to entice action (push strategy). A user will see something appealing to them, often while they go about a somewhat unrelated activity; for example, just browsing through to stay in touch with friends and family. Your role is to create something of interest and of value that they act upon.

- **Instagram:** designed to both entice action when seen and intercept people's search behaviours by way of a hashtag. Like Facebook, a good ad will appeal to someone scrolling through their Instagram feed, and will cause them to act in some way. The use of hashtags in posts can also intercept people who are searching, viewing or following various hashtags that are of interest to them. If you use hashtags it is likely your content can and will be found by people who are interested in it.

- **Google (and other search engines) paid and organic:** designed to respond to someone's search behaviours or actions. This is the opposite to the above: people are deliberately acting in a particular way when they come to Google. They are searching for something, looking at images, finding products or seeking answers. Your job is to ensure you are present when they are looking for whatever it is they are trying to find.

- **Electronic direct mail:** is purely a push strategy (although the sign up to the EDM or the content is typically a pull strategy). This means that the person *wants* to be exposed to what you have to say: your offers, your content, your news, your events, and so on. The flipside of this is when you procure a qualified database and then use this for cold contacts through EDM, in an attempt to drive traffic to a site, arrange a phone call, or similar.

My closing notes in this chapter are simple.

While you can do all this in-house, this is one of the biggest mistakes I see businesses make. They get lured by the free tools, free platforms, the "Facebook support" (a "dedicated account manager"), or a "Google ads specialist" to help them through the process. And sure, while this can be useful to get started, these people are not specialists in your business, nor will they take the time to genuinely understand the ins and outs of your audience.

To achieve the best results, you need an agency that has a dedicated team of specialists in each of the platforms, who have undergone training specific to that platform, and have also had extensive experience in establishing what works and what doesn't for a range of different industries and audiences. It is critical for the experts you employ to consistently keep up to date with the way the various platforms evolve and the changes they make to the way they work.

A CHECKPOINT

Using the notes section, determine which platform is most relevant to your audience and what strategies and tactics you could create to reach and engage them.

NOTES:

NOTES:

17

STEP 4: IMPLEMENT

You may have heard a saying along the lines of, "It's better to implement a plan and fail, than to not implement one at all". The point is, you can easily get paralysis by analysis when it comes to marketing. It's easy to get stuck in the planning phase, analysing all the data, creating the concepts and then getting stuck on the micro things, which honestly, I can guarantee no-one will ever pick up on.

You may have heard this one as well: "prolific beats perfect". In an era where content is king, and everyone is seeking answers, solutions and information on their problems, it's better to get it out there and test the market than to lose an opportunity. Regardless of the size of your business, being nimble and agile in these situations is key. Whether it be your team who is responsible for the activity or a third-party agency, you need to be able to test the market, see what they respond to, and then shift quickly from there.

I've already mentioned split testing your campaigns to establish which ad gets the best response. The same approach can apply with content. You will notice that many businesses, media houses and the like will publish content, and will then either re-purpose or re-publish that content at a later stage, with a different strapline, a different image or some other change. What they are doing is testing the combinations of graphics, video, taglines and so on to see which generates the best response. Ultimately the response governs what they do more of and less of.

HANDY THINGS TO KNOW

When it comes to implementation, I believe focus and consistency are key. Be strategic about getting your information and content out there. Look for engagement, response, feedback and attention. Here is a guide to use with digital channels that will help drive the implementation strategy:

- **Timing:** Timing is everything. Use the insights and data from your website, your social media and your emails to establish when your audience is primarily online.

- **Consistency:** Is there a commonality to your content, your style, your posts, your videos, and so on? Will your audience distinguish you and your business when they see it? Are you ensuring that whenever someone is exposed to your brand they will recognise it and feel connected?

- **Seasonality:** Are you aware of seasonal influences that could affect your campaign? What about dates or events that are important to your audience, such as holidays, Christmas or Mother's Day?

- **Relevancy:** Are you posting your content at times when your audience is likely to be consuming it, and is it relevant to that time of day (such as lunch breaks, or in the evening when the kids are in bed)? Has a major event happened that impacts your audience (such as storms, floods or changes in interest rates or legislation)?

- **Frequency:** Are you posting regularly to ensure you are being seen? And are you supporting this with paid "boosts" or ads? Are you regularly encouraging dialogue with your audience?

Another technique for your implementation strategy which should be considered is staggering the roll out of your campaigns, content and information over time so that you get a feel for the response. Again, this sounds like common sense, however too often I see businesses create five or six blogs and then post them all at once.

Staggering the campaigns or content also aids with the currency of what you are putting out there. For example, if you are releasing weekly blogs, Google will note that you have new content regularly being updated and will favour that content. The same applies with social media channels: the more current and the more relevant, the better.

Don't be afraid to get content out there. If you don't like the responses you receive, you can always take it down. The point is that you are implementing what you have created. You are taking the time to be of value to your audience, and that's what counts. You can use the feedback you receive to help you refine your content over time.

A CHECKPOINT
Using the notes section, start small and map out the next three months.

NOTES:

18

STEP 5: MEASURE

If there is one thing I love about the digital and social space more than anything, it's our ability to measure almost anything that happens online. Measuring is the core to all successful marketing. Without measurement, everything is just speculation and opinion. Unless you can link your activity back to your results with data, how can you draw reliable and quantifiable conclusions?

Of course, you need to ensure that each of your mediums and channels is set up correctly to accurately measure results. There are many basic measuring functions that are available to the majority of platforms, and they will provide enough information to enable you to at least seek professional advice and use that information to make considered decisions.

TOOLS FOR MEASURING ONLINE ACTIVITY

Great examples of the measuring tools that are freely available on the popular platforms are:

- **Google Analytics:** this is installed in your website and will analyse everything that happens on your site. It will allow you to measure paid traffic, organic traffic and referral traffic, and – for the advanced users – it allows you to set complex goals to suit your business and ROI needs.

- **Facebook Insights:** this provides you with a lot of data about your audience, where they are from, how many people "like" your page, reach engagement, and so on.

- **E-Commerce:** many e-commerce websites have the ability to track performance such as sales, enquiries, abandoned carts and repeat purchasing.

- **EDM software:** most email platforms allow you to measure the success of your emails, such as open rates, delete rates and unsubscribe rates.

- **Google AdWords (YouTube pre-roll, search, display, remarketing):** Google has a dedicated dashboard for reporting on the performance of all of your ad campaigns, presenting the key data relevant to the type of campaign.

- **LinkedIn:** has some stats about each of your posts and how they have performed, although it's still quite primitive. The advertising platform, on the other hand, isn't too bad, and measures enough to ascertain if your campaigns are performing well.

Further to this, many agencies and businesses use specific dashboards and reporting tools that help consolidate all the data into a single platform, so that they can help "tell a story" about what's happening across their channels at any given time.

As an agency, we use the CYFE dashboard. One of the most powerful and easy to use dashboards for recording and displaying critical data, it allows you to create "widgets", which are boxes of information that hold the data for each item you are measuring. If you are measuring a Facebook page and Google Analytics, CYFE will allow you to create those metrics in a single "dashboard".

UNDERSTANDING THE RESULTS

While having these metrics is one thing, understanding what they mean is another. There are a lot of great resources out there that outline the definitions of the metrics and help to make sense of what they mean. As a business owner or senior manager or marketer within an organisation, I believe you have a duty to understand the basics so that you can ask the right questions and understand the answers, to ensure you are getting the desired results and so that you know how to interpret the data.

Measuring plays a vital role in the calculations and decisions being made against the metrics and objectives that were set. As we covered in chapter 13, measuring ROI against each of the objectives is critical in establishing if the money being invested is generating the desired return.

As an agency, at this stage in the process we use this data to ascertain what we should do more (and less) of. It helps us to establish and understand a baseline for the investment, and allows us to establish that $X investment generates Y results. From there, we can use this information to scale. Accountability is key, and the only way we can be truly accountable is to let the data do the talking, and to use the information to guide future decisions.

The frequency of measurement should also be considered. The activities in place will determine how often reports should be generated. With our agency we always offer monthly reporting.

A snapshot of the month's actions provides a great insight into what we have achieved and delivered over the period. We also tend to do quarterly and annual reviews. A critical component of assessing the success of a campaign is benchmarking it and demonstrating the growth in the key metrics established. Often month-to-month activity is extremely volatile; what happens one month can be drastically different to the next. Regular reviews will enable you to detect and analyse such activity.

Often business owners or managers feel that they need to see everything "in the green" each month, but that's usually not the case (depending on the metric). A great example of why this is not always the case can be seen in activities such as engagement. Let's assume that one month you release a video, a piece of awesome content that repeatedly gets picked up, "liked", shared, viewed and commented on (you get the picture). When something takes on a life of its own online and gets spread organically, this is known as "virality" (when content goes viral). So you could imagine that if this happened one month and then the next month was the usual baseline activity, the numbers for the second month would be much lower; for example, one month reached one million people because of the video that went viral, and then the next month went back to normal, only reaching 50,000 people. This of course isn't a bad thing; it just means that one month a particular activity yielded excellent results, and then the next month things normalised. This is why data needs to be evaluated over longer periods of time, and why digital and social strategies typically have long-term goals broken down into smaller chunks and evaluated regularly.

THE BIGGER PICTURE

This also brings to light the importance of "telling a story" with the data at hand, and understanding that metrics shouldn't really be evaluated in isolation. The numbers need to be drawn together, understood and then translated into what this means for the business. How do these numbers relate to achieving the objectives that have been set? And what has been worthwhile, and what has under-performed, and why?

A CHECKPOINT

Using the notes section, write down all of the platforms you currently use or have in your business, and note down the data or information that each one can provide you with.

NOTES:

19

STEP 6: REFINE

It's one thing to persevere and hope for the best, that whatever you are doing is going to work, or to attempt to stick it out despite what the data is telling you. It's another to use the data – the output from the measurement of your digital marketing and social media activities – to establish if what you are doing is in fact working or if it requires some refinement.

Refinement to me is typically not a drastic change of strategy; that would more so be a strategy evaluation where it is established that a campaign has been successful (or unsuccessful) through whatever metrics have been chosen. Refinement is about the little things. It's what you do each month to ensure your campaigns, content and tactics are performing well, and optimising them in a way that makes them valuable and continually successful month after month.

THE BACK-END WORK

Often what is unseen in digital deliverables is the back-end work that goes into the results each month. Let's take a look at some of the strategies and the involvement that should occur frequently for your activities to be successful on an ongoing basis.

Facebook

There are two main elements to Facebook refinement. The first is content/placement refinement, and the second is advertising refinement.

Content/placement refinement

This is when you evaluate your content strategy from the month or months prior. You see what worked and what didn't. What did your followers comment on? What did they just "like"? Did they share a post? Or did you get really low reach? What time of day did you post? What sort of content was it? Did you try posting different types of content, such as images, videos and GIFs? Did your followers "like" the "sales" posts, or did they prefer interesting, engaging, funny or educational posts? Understanding the answers to these questions will allow you to refine your content and your placement strategy.

There are rules of thumb that are typically followed when it comes to content mix (though there are many varying opinions); for example, if the split between "interesting/engaging/educational" type posts and "sales type" posts is about 60/40, you basically give more than you take. But on some of the pages we manage we see that equation flipped on its head: the audience wants to see what products are coming out, and are less interested in any other content.

This is why refinement is so important. If you aren't giving your audience what they want then you are wasting your time and money. Refining your content ultimately means adjusting the type of content (the mix referred to above), and the refining of placement means adjusting the dates, times and location.

Advertising refinement

This is where you evaluate the performance of your paid campaigns and ascertain if they are performing well and generating the right returns for the investment. The primary method of doing this is to understand the cost of the result you are achieving based on your ad spend (as discussed in chapter 13). For example, if you are trying to build "likes" you will get a "cost per like", or if you have set "website traffic" as a goal you will get "cost per website views/ clicks", and so on. This is why, as explained earlier, your budget is so important. If, for example, you find that it's costing you $5.00 per "like", it could be a very expensive exercise trying to grow a decent following on your page. Or you might find that you pay $1.00 per website click, and the action they take on your website results in you obtaining their information, or perhaps even converts into an immediate sale – then that investment could well be worth scaling.

The other part of ongoing refinement is monitoring the campaigns and ensuring that the audience and the response to the ads is performing well. We mentioned split testing before, and that's a key component of testing the way your audience responds to an ad. This requires daily review and tweaking to ensure that you are putting your absolute best ad strategy forward.

SEO

Without opening up a can of "SEO worms", there are a number of things that require regular monitoring, evaluation and refinement. The assumption here is that the technical side (code and structure) of your website has been developed in a way that is congruent with

Google's expectations. Let's have a look at how you can refine your SEO:

- **Organic keywords/phrases:** What words or phrases are you currently being found with? Are these the terms that your audience knows or relates to? How are you using these in your content creation? Or, are you not being found at all?

- **Content:** Does the content on your site answer the questions your audience is asking? Is it updated regularly? Is it relevant to the searches being conducted? Is it a mix of blogs, videos and other content? Is it longer content articles for your topics on the website? Does it included tagged images? Do you have videos? Is your content meta-tagged?

- **Authority:** Are you present on the relevant directories? Have you asked other companies to link their websites back to your content? Is your content getting out there and driving traffic back to your site? Are you actively promoting and advertising your content through social media channels?

- **Listings:** Are you present on the relevant business directories? Do you have a Google+ Business Page? Have you set up your business on the most relevant social media channels?

Google AdWords

Google AdWords is a platform that requires regular optimisation and tweaking. The reason for this is that people's behaviours and searches change regularly. Google AdWords specialists study for years to keep up to date with the tools and techniques available to them when running AdWords campaigns.

The bottom line for Google AdWords is that if you aren't an expert then you should get some help if this is going to be a significant tool for managing your campaign. The amount of money you can waste attempting to make it work for you can be significant.

Google AdWords refinement typically requires you to ask questions such as:

- Have you established all of the negative keywords that you *don't* want to generate traffic to your ads?

- Have you ascertained if keywords are broad, exact, or phrase matched?

- Have your retargeting/remarketing lists been built yet? How large is that list?

- Have you connected your campaign to Google Analytics?

- Have you set the right conversion goals to accurately measure campaign performance?

- Is the copywriting in your ads appealing to your audience? Does Google rank this as relevant?

- Is your relevancy score acceptable?

- Is your budget appropriate for what you are competing on? Or would an increase in budget yield a better and more appropriate result?

- Are your display ads performing well on the right page placements?

- Which keywords or phrases are converting?

- Which keywords are driving traffic but *not* converting, and why?

- Is your budget being split appropriately? Should some words be allocated a higher budget than others?

- Has your geography been set appropriately? Is your budget enough for the allocated geography you have chosen?

- Is the place where Google is sending your traffic appropriate and relevant to what a user is looking for?

Website

Your website typically underpins all of the above activities. It becomes the "central hub" for all of your activity between the key channels and your efforts that you allocate to them.

By now you would get the picture that a website is not a "set and forget" tool, that you build once to tick a box and then you leave it to "do its thing". It doesn't work like that. A website is a business tool that is designed to capture an audience and motivate them to act in a particular way.

Refinement on a website should be considered, and the following questions asked:

- Are you regularly updating the content on your website?

- Are you regularly posting new content to your website?

- Are you adjusting your banners on your website to suit what people are coming to your site for?

- If you are running campaigns through other channels, is it evident when a user comes back to your site?

- Is all of your content tagged properly?

- Has your site map been submitted to Google?

- Does your website link to useful sources or to your other channels?

- Is it easy to get in contact with you and are you giving enough to your audience to entice them to contact you?

- On your site is it easy for users to find what they are after?

- How old is your website? Could it use a refresh or re-skin?

For most businesses there isn't a need to review or refine a website daily; every two or three months will suffice, subject to your level of activity and marketing. If for example you run monthly specials for your products and promote them through social media, you will want to ensure that people see this when they come to the website.

KEEPING IT SIMPLE

Refinement of your digital marketing and social media activity doesn't have to be an arduous task. It's about doing the little things regularly, and not allowing things to spiral out of control to a point where it takes a mass overhaul to get everything back on track. The analogy is it's like maintaining a car: most cars shouldn't need to be checked under the bonnet every day. But it does require regular petrol to run, or a top up of oil and other important lubricants, or a wash every week or two. If you apply these principles to all of your marketing and social media strategies you will find that your costs are easier to manage, you can be more accountable for your activity, and your audience will love you for it.

We have all interacted with a business that does this terribly; the restaurant, for example, that never updates its opening and closing hours between summer and winter. You rock up and the place is closed. Or the business that has prices on the website from three years ago. You know the ones.

The digital world drives you to be accountable. And so it should – it's easy to be guilty of not doing these simple things. Heck, I've been guilty in my businesses of doing the same thing (at times to the point where it's almost the "mechanic's car" or the "builder's house" scenario).

Just try it, a little each day, each week, each month, each year.

A CHECKPOINT

Keep things simple and use the notes section to identify some of the questions raised in this chapter, and consider ways in which you can refine your current activities.

NOTES:

PART V

EXECUTION (READY, AIM, FIRE)

20

THE FOLLOW THROUGH

Have you learnt enough to be dangerous?

Do you feel that you are ready now to take on the right exper-tise, resources and strategies, and invest in your digital marketing and social media actions with confidence?

Have you considered the kinds of conversations you might have with a prospective marketing executive you're looking to employ, or an external agency? Or maybe you are already working with an agency and you have some questions for them?

Reading this book is all well and good, but you won't get any value from it unless you take something from it and action it. I trust that you will come away with a greater understanding that leads you into in-depth and robust discussions about your digital marketing and social media strategies. Perhaps you might even give a copy of this book to prospective sales, marketing, finance and admin employees in your business to help them understand the journey and the "do's and don'ts" of digital marketing and social media strategy. After all, everyone needs to be committed. The digital marketing and social media process is designed to create demand, community, interest, engagement and conversion. Everyone on the team has a role to play in this. The expectation should be that you are all going on a journey together within the business; everyone is on the same bus.

I have seen many occasions, both through my employed marketing years and my agency marketing years, when one individual has been tasked with the digital marketing and social media activities. It tends to be a lonely road if their peers, colleagues and stakeholders aren't joining them on the journey. You don't need everyone to be banging the marketing drum in time to your illustrious beat, you just need to help them understand the importance of what you're doing, and help them buy into the journey.

This understanding will only be derived through pointed education, an education on the process holistically from beginning to end. From understanding the need to invest, and treating your actions as an investment, through to executing and refining what you are doing, and ensuring it is always relevant to your audience.

WHERE TO NOW?

If you are at a point in reading this where you are thinking, "Okay, where to from here?", take a little time out and ask yourself the following 10 key questions. Hopefully, if my book has made sense to you, each of these questions should be easy (or at least easier than it previously was) to answer:

1   Are you aware of the mistakes you may have made, and the problems you have encountered to date, surrounding your digital marketing and social media efforts?

2   Do you know what objectives you want to achieve in your business? Is it sales growth, market penetration, dominance in one industry, or perhaps simply attaining data and research to make your next strategic decision?

3   Do you have an understanding of the timeframe in which you would like to achieve your objectives? In what timeframe would you like to see these changes and achievements take place? Is it a 3, 6, 9, 12 or 24-month plan?

4   Do you have an appropriate budget to invest? If so, what budget do you have to allocate to these activities? Is it a conservative budget, or is it a generous one?

5   Do you know where your business currently stands? What is your "current state"? What is the baseline or benchmark of your business at present? For example, are you getting "x" number of leads or sales each day without really doing anything? Understanding this will influence the way in which you scale.

6   Are you prepared (and able) to handle any growth generated by the increased demand for your products or services through your digital marketing and social media activity?

7   Are you acutely aware of your target audience, who they are and what they want?

8   Do you believe your existing or prospective customers could be taken on a better journey towards the sale or upsell?

9   Are you aware of what you need to evaluate in deciding how much you take on in-house and how much you outsource to a third-party agency?

10 Do you understand the key metrics that should be attached to your digital marketing and social media efforts, and how they relate to the objectives being set?

If you have answered *yes* to most (if not all) of these questions, and you have some substance behind your thoughts, you're in a great position to move forward and begin doing your due diligence on the best way to proceed.

You should know by now what is and isn't appropriate, and have a fair understanding if someone is attempting to pull the wool over your eyes or genuinely knows their stuff. Hopefully this book has allowed you to look objectively at the digital marketing and social media process, and ultimately how it relates to your business, your audience and your perfect customer, how they behave, and how best to appeal to them. For some of you this book may well confirm that your efforts to date are aligned with the market, and conversely for others you might also understand what isn't necessary for your organisation.

In closing, I genuinely hope that I have instilled a level of knowledge and confidence in you, understanding that you have already been successful in business to date, yet are now armed with great insight to take you to the next level, or to at least adopt new digital marketing and social media strategies that you previously may not have engaged in.

A CHECKPOINT
Use the notes section to establish your next steps. Set a time to achieve them, and then go and get it done!

NOTES:

NOTES:

NOTES:

NOTES:

NOTES:

NOTES:

NOTES:

NOTES:

ACKNOWLEDGEMENTS

To my Mum and Dad – it goes without saying. You sacrificed so much for us as children to provide us with enough to get a good start in life. Mum, with your focus on education, you set the standard for learning and helped us value knowledge. And Dad, the work ethic you instilled in all of us, the attention to detail, pride in workmanship and discipline set me in good stead to perform and succeed. Thank you for never pushing me down a path or trying to live your lives vicariously through us. Thank you for showing us that it's okay to make mistakes as long as we own them, while setting our moral fabric. And – most importantly – thank you for loving us unconditionally.

Brian Scrymgeour, thank you for your influence, your life lessons that you somehow managed to massage into engineering lessons. Thank you for never stroking my ego, for saying it how it is, for telling me to pull my head in when I needed to, for always shedding light on the many sides of a situation, for always providing a listening ear, and a human approach to everything life threw at me. May you rest in peace. I miss you every day, and even more so now, as lonely and as hard as it gets sometimes. Thank you for being a mentor, confidant and friend.

Carlos Broens, I don't think I ever truly expressed my gratitude for the opportunity you gave me in not only starting my career, but allowing me to transition it. Your leadership and business style made a lasting impact in my life, whereby your philosophies, values and approach are engrained in the way I do business today. You saw something in me when others didn't. You opened up doors, giving me an exposure to business experience that was well beyond my years. Thank you for the bottles of red wine we shared on business trips, thank you for your humble approach to doing business, thank you for teaching me the power of silence, and most of all, for always going against the grain of what traditional industry did, while you paved a path for education, training, and development, while integrating technology without the expense of jobs.

Terry Benitez – best man, friend and mentor. You came into my life at a time when a friend was needed more than ever. You took me under your wing, taught me what was worth valuing and what wasn't. You gave me time, you had patience, you taught me how to enjoy life and appreciate what we have, the powers of alchemy, and how to turn something of less value into great value. I know we don't see each other enough, but when we do, it's like we caught up yesterday. Thank you for your eternal wisdom, kindness and friendship.

Dale Brittain, thank you for being the one genuine person (and agency) that went out on a limb to help me during a time when I was trying to cement my position and make an impact in the corporate world. Thank you for supporting me in my personal and professional endeavours, providing me with an opportunity to do business with you, to partner with you and to learn from you. Thank you for showing me what it takes to succeed in business, the foundations for relationships, and learning to understand and listen to clients. Your reputation is enviable, your industry stewardship an inspiration.

Peter Henry and Suzanne Haddan, from a business friendship has blossomed our most treasured family relationship. Thank you Peter for always having a listening ear, for your wisdom, your insight, your generous and supportive nature, your strategic mind, and most importantly, being a mate when I needed one. Thank you Suzanne, on a personal level for always being so welcoming, hospitable and loving towards my family, bribing our girls with Tic Tacs, and always being willing to give Danielle and me time to ourselves. And on a professional level, for your intelligence, unparalleled industry experience, advice and insight you've shared with me. You've achieved professional success that I could only dream of. Thank you to you both.

Andrew Handosa, my European buddy, bromance, karaoke partner. Thank you for being the listening ear that can challenge me, for helping me to celebrate and acknowledge the hustle. For being the guy that doesn't take a conversation on face value; who thinks, and then responds with intent. For your intellect, attitude, and unbelievably well adjusted view on life and what's really important. You've taught me more than you know; you've helped me in ways you wouldn't realise. I'm proud to call you a mate and I love watching everything you've done and continue to do in business.

Ali Akbarian, purveyor of critical and strategic thinking, master chef and BBQ/smoker chief, entertainer, consumer of fine wine and scotch, thank you for always supporting me and never being scared to challenge me. Thank you for our robust and intellectual discussions, as well as being able to just talk rubbish. For your hospitality and welcoming nature. Your work ethic is unquestionable, your focus on culture is admirable, and your impact on community and industry is exceptional.

Craig Hailston, accountant extraordinaire, business mentor, financial god – thank you for always making decisions in my best interest, from day one helping me accumulate a financial education, helping me understand my numbers and ensuring my businesses grows strongly and successfully. Thank you for taking the nonsense out of things, for being more than just an accountant, and having an excellent ability to see more than just numbers and being able to look at all facets of business.

James Morrell – coder, start-up investor, coffee lover. Thank you for being there since day one of my businesses. For being a lateral thinker, for always reflecting on what's being said and always coming back with valuable insight. Thank you for getting me out of jams, for working around the clock when the heat was on, for always being available, both professionally and personally. I value your insight and input immensely.

Danielle, Isabelle, Elloise and Xavier – my dear family. You are my rock. My inspiration. My reason to get out of bed even when I don't feel like it. My happiness in all that I do comes from you. Danielle, you are nothing short of a saint. Without you I could never have done what I have; you gave me the space to write my book, and the support to keep our family humming along while I work long hours. Thank you for always providing insight into people, personalities and relationships, and although you feel that you can't offer a lot when it comes to business, you offer more than you realise when it comes to people, and that to me is of immense value. Thank you for never wavering, and for working tirelessly to keep a beautiful home, happy children, and a strong and safe environment for us all to thrive in.

INDEX

A

"above the line" marketing 52, 84
A/B split testing 79, 113
action mistakes 31–32
ad campaigns 137
AdSense 150
AdWords 32, 36–37, 149–152, 166, 174–175
aggregators 69
articles 66, 69
Australian Bureau of Statistics (ABS) 133
Australian Financial Review 78

B

barriers to entry 16
blackhat techniques 153–154
brand awareness 59, 63–72, 118–120
— measuring 63–65
brand names 118
budget 14, 103–125
— allocating 14, 109
budgeting 12, 20–30, 79, 103–125
business to business (B2B) 50
business to consumer (B2C) 50

C

calendars 69
call to action (CTA) 137, 144
channels to market 58, 78
chapter checkpoints 40, 46, 53, 61, 72, 81, 93, 100, 109, 114, 125, 133, 140, 158, 169, 177, 184
checklists 69
common mistakes 29–40
— learning from 29–31
competitors 1, 12, 13, 57

content 58, 78, 138, 174
— creating 143–158
— curating 154–155
— definition of 68–72
— importance of 64–67
— placement of 172–173
content strategies 39
conversion 123, 145
copywriting 175
cost per acquisition 121–122
cost per click 119, 173
cost per conversion 123–124
cost per lead 23, 122–123
current customers 132
customer expectations 46
customer experience 46
CYFE dashboard 167

D

databases 21–23, 77, 97, 136
— building 138
data gathering 25, 130–133
demographics 52
digital-only campaigns 113
driving action 67

E

earned channels 61
eBay 78, 150, 151
ebooks 69
e-commerce websites 166
electronic direct mail (EDM) 137, 155–157, 166
email subject lines 155
engagement 59, 83–93
— measuring 90–91
engaging friends and family 32, 39–40
e-word of mouth 92
expert tips 69
"eyeballs" 68

F

Facebook 36–38, 78, 79, 80, 83, 90–91, 98, 131, 148, 156
— creating content for 145–147
— doing it yourself 32
— number of users 88–89
— purchasing likes 91
— refining strategy 172–173
— size of following on 32
Facebook Insights 99, 166
followers 90–93, 98

G

geographic data 52
getting started 20, 109, 181–184
gifs 70
Gitomer, Jeffrey 57
glossaries 69
goal setting 20–26, 97
Google 32, 78, 80, 119–120, 148–155, 157
— algorithm 36–37
— blacklisting by 37, 154
— doing it yourself 32
— ranking on 119, 154
Google AdWords 97
Google Analytics 96–97, 99, 130–131, 166, 175
Google+ Business Page 174
Gumtree 78, 150, 151

H

hashtags 148, 156
"how to" guides 69

I

IBISWorld 130, 132
implementation 161–163
impressions 68
in-depth guides 69
industry bodies 132–133
industry reports 130
infographics 69
Instagram 83, 90, 148, 156
interviews 70
investing in your business 105–106

K

keywords 131, 149, 150, 152, 174, 175

L

lead generation 59, 75–81, 137
— process of 76–79
— purpose of 75
leads 75–81
— cost of 23, 122–123
"likes" 32, 90–91, 98, 173
— purchasing 37–38
LinkedIn 89–90, 147–148, 156, 166
listicles 70
long-term strategies 137–139
loyalty 92

M

marketing
— accountability and 107–108
— analysing 129–133
— certainty and 107
— common problems with 11–16
— definition of 49
— different aspects of 2
— frustration with 1–7, 12–13
— language of 46–50
— monitoring and measuring 79, 165–169
— optimising 79
— refining 79, 171–177
— sales and 58
— strategies 112–114
— tactics 2
— testing 79
— tools 15
— traditional 13, 84
— uncertainty about 15
— understanding 3, 46–50
— value and 108
marketing agencies 3, 16, 43–46, 112
— selecting 44–45
market research 64, 84–85
mass audiences 16
media blasts 137
memes 70
meta-tagging 174
mobile devices 78

N

new entrants to market 12, 13
news 70

O

objectives 16–26, 58–59, 77, 95
— importance of 19–26
— return on investment and 117–121
one-way communication 83–84
online community 59
— building 138
— understanding 83–93
online platforms
— free 16, 38–39, 59–60
— paid 59–60
online stores 21–22
online traffic 59, 175
organic traffic 119, 174
outsourcing 16
— overseas 32, 36–37
owned channels 60

P

paid, owned, earned 59–61
pay per click (PPC) 137
PDF downloads 70
people to people (P2P) 50–51
"pixels" 80
podcasts 70
power of the customer 85–88
pre-roll ads 150, 166
product reviews 70
products and services 46, 51, 78–81
profiling methodology 52–53, 77
profit per sale 124
promotion 93
psychographic data 52
"push strategies" 58, 84

R

ratings 92
real-world communities 93
rebranding 138
recipes 70
referral traffic 97–98, 137

remarketing 79–80, 151, 166, 175
research papers 70
resources 12, 15–16, 23
results 20, 117–125, 167–171
— measuring 22–23
retargeting 79–80, 151, 175
return on investment 117–125, 167–171
— calculating 120–124
— objectives and 117–121
reviews 92

S

sales 57–61
search engine optimisation (SEO) 36–37,
   98, 173–174
— organic 152–154
— overseas companies and 32
search engines 157
short-term strategies 136–137
SMART goals 20–26
"snacking" on content 147
Snapchat 83
social media 58
— analysing 129–133
— common problems with 11–16
— different aspects of 2
— frustration with 1–7, 12–13
— gathering data from 131–132
— managing in house 38–40
— monitoring and measuring
   165–169
— refining 171–177
— strategies 112–114
— tactics 2
— tools 15
— uncertainty about 15
— understanding 3
social media agencies 3, 16, 43–46,
   112–114
— selecting 44–46
socioeconomic data 52
split testing 79, 113
Squarespace 31
straplines 155
strategic marketing approach 2

T

tables 70
tactics 31–35
target audience 20, 38–39, 65, 77, 88–90, 162
— identifying 33–34, 78
— level of engagement of 38–39
— providing value to 66–68, 71–72
target customers 16, 76–77
— identifying 20–22, 49–53
thinking mistakes 31–32
three dominant problems 14–16
timeframes 23, 25–26, 70, 136–140
"touches" 79–80, 136
trade shows 137
traditional marketing 13, 84
traffic 59, 119, 137, 174, 175
— monitoring 96–100
— sources of 97–98
— understanding 95–100
transcriptions 71
tutorial videos 71

Twitter 83, 90
two-way communication 58, 83–84, 90–93

V

views 68, 80, 146, 148, 150
— cost of 173

W

waste 16, 52–53
websites 35–36
— content for 144–145, 176–177
— doing it yourself 31
— gathering data from 130–131
— goals for 97, 99–100, 144, 156
— number of hits 23, 96–97
Whereis 151
whitehat techniques 153
Wix 31, 44

Y

YouTube 13, 95, 150, 166